A Philosophy of the Human Being

Julian A. Davies

University Press of America,® Inc.
Lanham · Boulder · New York · Toronto · Plymouth, UK

⊖™ The paper used in this publication meets the minimum
requirements of American National Standard for Information
Sciences—Permanence of Paper for Printed Library Materials,
ANSI Z39.48—1984

TABLE OF CONTENTS

PREFACE

This book is the outcome of a necessity and a revelatory moment. The necessity was a project for sabbatical. The revelation came when passing out handouts with selections from philosophers and ensuing student confusing about which was which. Having taught the Philosophy of the Human Being over a number of years, using several texts, I thought it is time to write my own text.

One of the goals of the text was to have significant quotations from the philosophers in the text itself. Another goal was to make a readable text, as free as possible from superfluous background in the History of Philosophy and focused on issues. A third goal was to have some contemporary, almost popular style, readings in the text to complement my own presentation. Adding review questions to the chapters and readings was something I had also long been doing in my classes and intended to continue doing.

After describing to the reader what philosophy is, and what it isn't, and discussing the topic of presuppositions and the particular presuppositions of this text, I treat in successive chapters, human sociability, intelligence, freedom, duality, individuality/personhood, and immortality. A final chapter looks over each of those topics and pushes the topics further in support of the overall position of the text, a realistic dualism as contrasted to materialism.

Aristotle is probably the most often quoted primary source, though Plato gets his due too. I have worked into text some citations from secondary sources that seem to me to have said precisely what I wanted to say with a different voice. I chose not to begin the book with Thales and the early Greeks, but rather to give the readers a taste of Plato as a start in philosophy. Although I have used Plato's *Apology* (the one reading not embedded, but easily accessible) as a start, the *Euthyphro*, or *Crito* might prove as useful an introduction to philosophical thinking.

Again, I have used Plato as an example of the rationalistic approach to knowledge; some might prefer to use Descartes for that purpose. I have selected Lucretius as my main spokesmen for materialism, seeing in his views fewer philosophical presuppositions that would complicate the issues for a beginner in philosophy.

Although placed in an appendix, the brief treatment of Definition and Rules for Definition is something I have found valuable in itself; and as a vehicle for review of presented material.

I found a great deal of enjoyment in writing this little book and hope that students and others reading it do so too.

Fr. Julian Davies, O.F.M.
Siena College, Loudonville, New York
October 21, 2008

ACKNOWLEDGMENTS

Coming out of a text book tradition, I wish to honor the late Fr. Joseph Donceel, S.J., and Fr. James Reichmann, S.J., whose works inspired and aided me in my efforts. I wish to make special mention of the late Dr. Larry Azar. I only recently came to know his work, and I am grateful for the permission to cite several long excerpts from his superb text: *Man: Computer, Ape or Angel?*

I give special thanks to Siena College for granting me the sabbatical leave to write this book. Special thanks also to Fr. Cassian Miles, O.F.M., whose editor's eye caught many a typo and unclear pronoun reference. The book is a much improved work because of his efforts. Also thanks to Sue Kuebler of Siena's Faculty Support Office who helped greatly with the manuscript, and to Sharon Gariepy who prepared the camera-ready copy. Finally, thanks to the staff of the University of America Press who steered me through this process to publication.

TEXT ACKNOWLEDGMENTS

Adler, Mortimer J., Excerpts from *Ten Philosophical Mistakes*. Reprinted with the permission of Scribner, a Division of Simon & Schuster Adult Publishing Group from TEN PHILOSOPHICAL MISTAKES by Mortimer J. Adler. © 1985 by Mortimer J. Adler. All rights reserved.

Aristotle, Excerpts from BARNES, JONATHAN, BASIC WORKS OF ARISTOTLE ©1988 Princeton University Press, 1988. Reprinted by permission of Princeton University Press.

Azar, Larry, Excerpts from *Man: Computer, Ape or Angel?* © Larry Azar. Hanover, MA. Christopher Publishing Co., 1985. Reprinted with permission of Patricia Azar.

Kreeft, Peter. Excerpt from "The Best Things in Life" by Peter Kreeft. Copyright © 1984 Intervarsity Press Fellowship/USA. Used with permission of Intervarsity Press, P.O. Box 1400, Downers Grove, IL 60515. Ivpress.com.

Peters, John A. Excerpts from *Metaphysics: A Systematic Survey* by John A. Peters. Duquesne Studies Philosophical Series VII. 16, Pittsburgh, PA. Duquesne University Press, 1963. Reprinted with permission.

Plato, Excerpts from HAMILTON EDITH. THE COLLECTED DIALOGUES OF PLATO INCLUDING THE LETTERS © 1961 Princeton University Press, 1989 renewed. Reprinted with permission of Princeton University Press.

Chapter 1

THE PHILOSOPHY OF PHILOSOPHY

WHAT IS PHILOSOPHY?

There are many comical definitions of philosophy. One that I like is this: "Philosophy is the subject which talks about what everybody knows in language that nobody knows." The first part of the definition is true, the second part is exaggerated. Philosophy does talk about things we all know—about human beings, their freedom and intelligence, their destiny after life, their specific trademark such as using language and inventing machines and constructing civilizations. Philosophy also talks about moral standards and principles and philosophy talks about God too.

So philosophy does discuss ideas that people have an acquaintance with. And sometimes its language is ponderous, obscure and, to the amateur, approaching double-talk. However, every subject has its jargon—its technical terms that in context make sense—say, "supply-chain management" in business, and "atrial fibrillation" in the medical milieu. Most readers of this book have learned computer jargon—hardware and software, megabytes, and gigabytes, and so forth. The problem with philosophical jargon is there is so much of it. Philosophers tend to create new words to express their new or thought-to-be-new ideas.

However there is no need to panic. There are a limited amount of questions and ideas that preoccupy philosophers, Philosophers discuss whether there is a God, and come up with different names for that ultimate reality. One calls God "Pure Act", another, the "Good:" another, "The One." The idea is the same. When speaking of freedom some call defenders of freedom "voluntarists," others "self-determinists," some "moderate indeterminists." Again, the meaning is the same.

The word "philosophy" comes from a Greek word meaning "love of wisdom." A "search for explanations" is perhaps a better description of what philosophers do. Why is there something rather than nothing? How do humans differ from animals? What happens after death? These kinds of questions look for an understanding of what lies beyond or beneath the surface of everyday life, and hence, philosophy has the reputation of a "deep" subject. Sometimes it is deep, to be sure, but it is seldom inaccessible.

We can now define philosophy: *an organized branch of human knowledge which attempts a fundamental explanation of reality by thinking and dialogue.* In this definition we find a description of what philosophy studies, the goal of its study, the point of view from which it studies, and the method it employs. What is studied is reality—God, humans, the world. Hence we have three branches of philosophy, Philosophy of God, or Natural Theology, Philosophy of the Human Being, often called Rational Psychology, and Philosophy of the World, Cosmology. There is an area of philosophy that looks to treat God, humans, and the world together and looks for general principles or concepts that could embrace them all. Such a study is called Philosophy of Being or Metaphysics, a name that suggesting its study is something beyond and above the physical.

Another area of reality is the realm of values—ethical, political, logical, aesthetic. Studies in such areas are often labeled *practical*, since their purpose is to learn how to act morally, establish society, reason correctly, or create beauty. The philosophical areas that study the nature and existence of God, the traits of the human being, the origin and ultimate make up of the world are called *speculative*, because they seek understanding for its own sake, not for some specific useful purpose. This contrast between speculative philosophy and practical philosophy is similar to a corresponding contrast in the physical sciences. For example Physics is a theoretical or speculative science which studies principles of bodies, and Engineering, which studies the application of those principles, is a practical science. Biology is a speculative science and Medicine is a practical science.

The words "fundamental explanation" express the goal of philosophy. As we indicated in the previous paragraph, philosophy looks for the "Why" of things. The word "fundamental" suggests the differences between the philosophical search for explanation and the scientific search for explanation. Philosophers look for ultimate or basic explanations, scientists, for immediate ones. For example, scientists explain language by describing the role of lips, teeth, tongue, larynx and diaphragm in speech; philosophers explain language as a function of human intelligence, a distinguishing trait of humans. When it comes to explaining the universe, science must begin with matter, whereas philosophy asks the question "Where does matter come from?" It is worth noting that practical philosophy, too, looks to discover fundamental principles, underlying reasons. The logician, for instance, seeks the general rules that govern correct reasoning, and the ethicist, for moral principles that should guide human behavior. Both of these studies look for norms, rather than just describing the way people do think and act, as psychologists and social scientists do.

The word "human" in the definition of philosophy refers to the point of view of philosophy, the type of knowledge that it is. Philosophy is the result of the thought process and verbalization of human beings. Unlike a religion, philosophy does not derive its concepts and teachings from a sacred book, or Church. For instance, when the philosopher speaks about life after death, he builds up arguments which can be based on the nature of humans as spiritual, or the ethical demand that good be adequately rewarded and evil sufficiently punished. When a religion, speaks of life after life, it cites the words of Jesus, "He who believes in me has everlasting life," or the teaching of the Koran that the good live forever. To state it another way, in philosophy it is the compelling force of the argument itself which leads to conviction, whereas in religion, it is the compelling belief in the authority of the word of God and/or Church that generates conviction.

The words "thinking and dialogue" describe the method of philosophy. Philosophers reflect on things, write out their thoughts and publish them for others to critique. The philosophical mode of proof is argument, a good word in philosophy. Argument means setting forth in a coherent pattern convincing reasons for what you hold to be true. The use of this method—and this method alone—is another way that philosophy differs from science. Science's method is the experimental method. Observation, measurement, manipulation of its materials is the way of the sciences. Philosophy doesn't—and can't—do that for much of what it studies, human nature, the after-life, morals. There is no litmus paper test for the existence of God, or a spiritual soul. We cannot expect to find in philosophy physical proofs for ideas or principle, no "crucial experiments" that will test a philosophical theory.

An important consequence of philosophy's method will be a diversity of opinions in philosophy, sometimes even opposing opinions on the same matter. Historically, this has caused some philosophers to despair of ever knowing the truth and to embrace the view known as *Skepticism,* that *"No knowledge is attainable."* Skeptics overlook their logical inconsistency, for to say "No knowledge is attainable" is to claim knowledge, and to exhibit knowledge of the meanings of words. Skepticism also shows itself in the view known as relativism, a view as old as Protagoras claim that "Man is the measure of all things".[1] *Relativism* teaches that *all truth depends totally on individual perspective or, more frequently, society's viewpoint.* According to the first version of relativism if I understand the world is flat, then it is flat, if you see it as round, it is round. According to the second, if our society views marriage as the choice of the persons to be married, that is correct. If another society sees marriage as the choice of the parents of the bride and groom, that view too is correct. Relativism is like skepticism a self-contradictory view, since the claim "All is relative" is proposed as an absolute, universal truth. Furthermore, it makes the human quest for truth futile.

Newcomers to philosophy are sometimes disturbed by the conflicting opinions of philosophers, but they should remember that the human mind is capable of distinguishing good arguments from bad. Francis Bacon wrote in this regard, "Philosophy when studied, first inspires doubt, but when mastered, dispels doubt."[2]

So far we have described philosophy and distinguished it from science and religion. One question remains, "How does philosophy differ from a "philosophy of life"? A philosophy of life is a personal worldview consisting of a set of beliefs about the world and one's place in it, a set of moral standards, a collection of values and interests, and a chosen lifestyle. A philosophy of life is derived from a variety of sources—religion, culture, one's personal experience. A philosophy of life also includes large elements of choice, particularly in the matter of morals and lifestyle—vegetarian or meat-eater; drinker or non-drinker, for example. Philosophy is a more objective endeavor and is based on reason alone, not culture or religion, Philosophy considers general not personal experiences—the fact that people have emotions, rather than Dad's anger because the car has no gas. Finally, philosophy seeks to be based on the mind and evidence, rather than the power of choice. One holds that alcohol use is licit or illicit based on one's reasons, apart from a personal choice of drinking or not drinking.

For the sake of completeness, we need to expand our description of "reality." "Reality" does include our knowledge of it. And so philosophers reflect on the very idea of knowledge in a special study called Philosophy of Knowledge or Epistemology. Philosophy looks at particular branches of knowledge too, and so there are: Philosophy of History, Philosophy of Education, Philosophy of Physic, or the natural sciences collectively in Philosophy of Science. Our knowledge of activities is the subject of such philosophical subjects as Philosophy of Cooking, Philosophy of Acting, Philosophy of Basketball, or of any human activity. In all of these areas the philosopher seeks the underlying principles that explain and form the basis of the knowledge or activity.

An Outline of Philosophy

I. Speculative philosophy—looking for understanding for the sake of understanding, to satisfy the desire to know.
1. Philosophy of God, Natural Theology
2. Philosophy of the Human Being, Rational Psychology
3. Philosophy of the World, Cosmology
4. Metaphysics or Philosophy of Being
5. Philosophy of Knowledge, Epistemology.
6. Philosophy of a specific area of Knowledge, Philosophy of History, Philosophy of Education, Philosophy of Physics

II. Practical philosophy—looking for understanding in order to act.
1. Philosophy of Reasoning, Logic
2. Philosophy of Morality, Ethics
3. Philosophy of Art, Aesthetics
4. Philosophy of Society/Governing, Politics
5. Philosophy of any Human Activity, e.g. Philosophy of Cooling, Philosophy of Basketball, Philosophy of Acting

Presuppositions of Philosophy

Since philosophers look "to explain things everybody knows", they like to spell out what everybody takes for granted in every area of life and in particular areas of philosophic inquiry. Those conscious and unconscious assumptions we make are called presuppositions, and they may be facts, like the existence of human beings in society, or principles, like the Principle of Non-Contradiction that states," *A Being cannot exist and not exist at the same time from the same standpoint.*" The definition of a *presupposition* is: *"a statement or fact accepted as true because a) it*

*is self-evidently true without need of proof, b) it has been proved in an-
other branch of knowledge, or c) it is arbitrarily assumed. "*

The phrase "self-evidently true" means obvious, without need of any
proof. Facts such as the existence of the material world of earth and water, the reality of plants, animals and humans are obvious and need no
proof. There are also self-evident principles, like the previously stated
Principle of Non-Contradiction, whose truth is known just by thinking
about it. Also, this statement, "The whole is greater than any of its parts,"
which follows from the definition of whole and part, is such a principle.

The phrase "proved in another branch of knowledge" means just that.
Human knowledge builds on previous knowledge. Geometry, for example, presupposes Algebra; Biology in the twenty-first century presupposes Chemistry, All of Philosophy presupposes Logic.

The expression "arbitrarily assumed," does not mean capriciously or
haphazardly, but selected. Non-Euclidian geometry, for example, assumes that parallel lines can intersect. Mathematics can be done with
various bases. In the practical order, all games have their rules. If you are
playing baseball "Three strikes and you are out." is taken for granted, as
is "Six points for a touchdown" in football.

Three self-evident principles and two of their corollaries are so central to every branch of knowledge as well as philosophy that they deserve
further explanation. The first of these is the *Principle of Intelligibility*
that simply states: *"Reality is knowable. "* Anything that is real in any
way can be understood. This principle implies that all questions have
answers, even if we may not able to answer them now. Accordingly, it is
worthwhile to try to find cures for Cancer and AIDS, and to look for oil
beneath the sea.

The second self-evident principle is the earlier mentioned *Principle
of Non-Contradiction* (sometimes called the *Principle of Contradiction*)
which states that: *"A reality cannot exist and not exist at the same time
from the same standpoint. "* As a statement about knowledge, it reads: *"A
statement cannot be simultaneously true and false" in the same context, "*
or *"The same predicate cannot be simultaneously affirmed and denied of
the same subject. "* The insight behind this evident principle is that being
is not the same as nothing. Having money and not having it are different,
as are presence and absence. The *Principle of Non-Contradiction* tells us
that contradictory answers to the same question cannot both be right, and
that "You can't have your cake, and eat it too."

The third principle is *The Principle of Sufficient Reason*: which
states: *"Everything has an adequate explanation for existing and acting. "* Since being is not the same thing as nothing, if something does ex-

ist, something must explain why it exists. And if something acts in a certain way, that behavior can be explained. For instance, as we will see, humans use language, so there must be an adequate explanation for it, namely, that humans have minds capable of thinking abstractly.

The *Principle of the Relation of Action and Nature* is a corollary of the Principle of Sufficient Reason and it states: *"The activities of a being flow from and reveal its nature."* What a thing does, tells us what it is. If it grows and reproduces, it is alive. If it is inclined to be with other beings and communicate with them, it is social; if it lives in the water, it is a marine animal.

The *Principle of Proportionate Causality* is the second important corollary of the Principle of Sufficient Reason. It reads: *"Every effect has a cause adequate to produce it."* Using it, we conclude that an animal like a dog cannot compose music nor a pet rock reproduce pebbles.

THE PHILOSOPHY OF THE HUMAN BEING
AND ITS PRESUPPOSITIONS

Philosophy of the Human Being can be defined as: *"The human and philosophical study of the nature of the human being, that is the essential characteristics that make up human beings, and their manifestations and implications."* The word "human" refers to the fact that philosophy comes from human thought not from Divine Revelation through a Sacred Text or Tradition. The word "philosophical" suggests the type of reflective study philosophy is, as opposed to a scientific study. The word "nature of humans" means the reality that is shared by all humans. "Essential traits" are defining traits, and the defining traits singled out in this study are Intelligence, Freedom, Sociability, Duality, and Individuality. "Manifestations" are evidences that point to defining traits. For example, the fact that humans use language points to both their Intelligence and Duality. The fact that humans make friends and form families shows that they are social. "Implications" are consequences which flow from the defining traits. For instance, the trait of Duality means that humans have a spiritual part as well as a material part, and that implies immortality, for what is spiritual cannot die.

In addition to the Principles explain above, Philosophy of the Human Being has some special presuppositions, some of which have already been referred to. That area of Philosophy takes for granted the existence of human beings, and the reality of many types of human experiences, such as friendships, feelings, knowledge, freedom, language. These experiences are so evident they do not have to be proven.

Furthermore, Philosophy of the Human Being looks at human beings, men and women, to find the essential traits of humans. Because men and women constitute the human species biologically, culturally and socially, we presuppose that no *essential* difference in *humanity* exists between men and women. Both are sharers in an identical human nature, since both engage in activities of knowing, choosing, communicating, feeling, loving, which are activities that characterize humans. We recognize that among human beings, and among men in general and women in general, there are different ways of reaching a decision, knowing, feeling, interacting with others, but these differences, significant as they are, do not establish that men and women are essentially different beings, different species of reality.

From the realm of Logic, Philosophy of the Human Being draws two distinctions used throughout its investigations. First is the distinction between *difference of degree* and *difference in kind. A difference in degree occurs when two things compared have more or less of the same trait.*[3] For example, humans have varying capabilities of hearing, eyesight, intelligence, athletic and musical ability. It makes sense to say some have more or less of those traits. And the sight of an eagle is sharper than that of humans, and the sense of smell of a dog keener than humans, and a tree is taller than a blade of grass. All these are examples of difference in degree. *A difference in kind occurs when one being has an essential, that is, defining, trait that the other lacks.* Living beings have the ability to reproduce, non-living beings do not; accordingly, they differ in kind. Water and coal differ in kind, because coal has Carbon and water doesn't and coal is combustible and water is not. Humans, as we will see, differ in kind from animals by having free will (and other traits too) which animals do not have. However, as we suggested in our treatment of the Principle of Non-Contradiction, statements always have a context. Hence these differences, kind and degree, are not absolute measures, but must be situated. For example, men and women differ only in degree as regards their being human and in traits like intelligence, freedom, and sociability. But they differ in kind in regard to reproductive organs. Depending on one's point of view, one could argue a square and a rectangle differ in kind, or only in degree.

A second important distinction that comes from Logic is the difference between the *univocal use of a term, the equivocal use of a term*, and the *analogous use of a term. A term*, that is *a word or group of words with meaning,* is used *univocally when it is used with exactly the same meaning in different sentences*. For example, the term "tree" is used univocally in these sentences. "The oak is a type of tree" and "The elm is a type of tree". The word human is used univocally in the sentences, "Derek Jeter is a human," and "Cameron Diaz is a human." It is necessary when trying to prove a point, that words keep the same meaning, that they be used univocally throughout the course of an argument.

A word is used equivocally when it is used with *two different and unrelated meanings*. For example the word "box" is a noun referring to a four-sided container, and also is a verb meaning to engage in a fight according to rules. The word "light" means not heavy or that which gives illumination. "Bank" can mean the turning of an airplane, or a place to hold money. Equivocal use of terms is to be avoided in philosophy and any serious attempt at communication.

A word is used analogously when *it is used in a related, but not exactly the same meaning in two different statements*. Accordingly, the word "good" is used analogously in each of these three statements: "I have a good car," "I have a good friend," "I ate a good meal last night." Likewise the word "smart" is used analogously in these statements: "Fido is a smart dog." The military deployed a smart bomb. "John is a smart man." In the first set of statements, the word "good" suggests something desirable, but a car, a friend, and a meal are not desirable in exactly the same way. And although a dog, a bomb, and a man can all determine how to get where they are going, they are not smart in exactly the same way. When a term is used analogously, there will always be a similarity of meaning and a difference. Furthermore, the same word can be used univocally and analogously in different sets of propositions. The word "colorful" is used univocally in these sentences. "It was a colorful arrangement of flowers." And "The outfits they wore were colorful." Either one of those statements with this statement involves analogy, "He has a colorful personality." Likewise, when sugar and chocolate are both described as "sweet", that term is being used univocally. When sugar is described as sweet and a person is described as "sweet" that word is being used analogously.

Are there any relationships between these two sets of differences: difference in kind and difference in degree and univocal use of a term and analogous use of a term? When two things differ in kind, a word describing an essential trait of one thing cannot be applied to the other that does not have this trait, except analogously. Thus a live wire and a live dog differ in kind. If the wire has electricity it is described as "live" but only analogously because a dog has life in a different way. Again, when a computer is described as "intelligent" and a human is described as "intelligent," the word "intelligent" is used analogously, because humans and computers differ in kind, and differ in the kind of intelligence they have. For computers don't understand the information they store while humans do.

REVIEW QUESTIONS AND EXERCISES

1. What are the four main areas of philosophy? What are the names of philosophy courses that deal with those areas?
2. How does the distinction between speculative philosophy and practical philosophy parallel the distinction between theoretical and practical science?
3. How is philosophy similar to science, as well as different from it?
4. How is philosophy like and unlike religion?
5. What are some of the presuppositions of other courses you are taking?
6. How is skepticism self-contradictory?
7. What examples of difference in kind and difference in degree can you think of? Think of examples from your other courses.
8. Give at least three examples of univocal and analogous uses of terms, using words used in courses you are taking.

SOME QUESTIONS ON PLATO'S *Apology*

1. Using material from the text, give two ways in which Socrates defends himself against the charge of atheism.
2. Give Socrates' reasons for not fearing death.
3. Do you think Socrates believes in immortality?
4. What is your opinion of Socrates? Is he admirable or not?

NOTES

1.   Cited in Plato, *Theaetetus*, 152a.
2.   Francis Bacon.; source is unknown.
3.   See Mortimer Adler. *The Difference in Man and the Difference It Makes*.
(New York: Holt, Rinehart, and Winston, 1967), 19-23.

Chapter 2

HUMAN SOCIABILITY

Human beings are characterized by the variety and complexity of their relationships and their need for and delight in such relationships. Humans are born into families; reach out to form friends, play with, work with, and worship with others. Humans establish villages, cities, and nations. Humans form clubs, fraternal societies, and sororities, labor unions, and corporations, partnerships, and dealerships, sports teams, and armies. Humans evidently do things with others. Furthermore, humans feel lonely when cut off from others. Isolation from other people is a form of punishment in home, school, or prison.[1] Given that activities reveal the nature of a being, it follows that humans are naturally, essentially social beings, beings that are inclined to and desire and seek to interact with other humans.

In this Chapter we will discuss three of the indications of human sociability, the formation of civil society, friendship, and the creation of voluntary associations. We will also examine the vehicle that makes these three possible—human language.

SOCIETY

The philosopher Aristotle long ago reflected on the origin of civil society and governments, or states:

> The family is the association established by nature for the supply of men's everyday wants, and the members of it are called by Charondas, 'companions of the cupboard', and by Epimenides the Cretan, 'companions of the manger'. But when several families are united, and the association aims at something more than the supply of daily needs, the first society to be formed is the village. And the most natural form of

the village appears to be that of a colony from the family, composed of the children and grandchildren, who are said to be 'suckled with the same milk'. . . .

When several villages are united in a single complete community, large enough to be nearly or quite self-sufficing, the state comes into existence, originating in the bare needs of life and continuing in existence for the sake of a good life. And therefore, if the earlier forms of society are natural, so is the state, for it is the end of them, and the nature of a thing is its end. For what each thing is when fully developed, we call its nature whether we are speaking of a man, a horse, or a family. . . .

Hence it is evident that the state is a creation of nature, and that man is by nature a political animal. . . .

The proof that the state is a creation of nature and prior to the individual is that the individual, when isolated, is not self-sufficing; and therefore he is like a part in relation to the whole. But he who is unable to live in society, or who has no need because he is sufficient for himself, must be either a beast or a god: he is no part of a state. A social instinct is implanted in all men by nature, and yet he who first founded the state was the greatest of benefactors. For man, when perfected, is the best of animals, but, when separated from law and justice, he is the worst of all; since armed injustice is the more dangerous, and he is equipped at birth with arms, meant to be used by intelligence and excellence, which he may use for the worst ends. That is why, if he has not excellence, he is the most unholy and the most savage of animals, and the most full of lust and gluttony. But justice is the bond of men in states; for the administration of justice, which is the determination of what is just, is the principle of order in political society.[2]

Speaking from his experience of the city-state organization of Greece, and from what he had read about, Aristotle sees humans as born into families, really no great insight. He looks at family from a functional point of view—it enables humans to satisfy everyday needs, food, clothing, shelter. He does not go into the rich emotional satisfaction that family life can bring, for the topic of family is being treated as a step on the way to society. The next step is extended family, and villages, as any explorer or anthropologist knows. Villages are groupings of families in proximity to one another.

Groups of villages establish a larger society or state, for the reason of providing the necessities of life. There has to be a sufficient number of villages, so as to make the larger entity self-sufficient, or nearly so. Self-sufficient implies being able to protect its citizen from other humans, to produce enough food for all, to assist its citizens in managing the forces of nature and assist them in times of natural disasters. States have another important purpose for humans, a purpose that keeps them going, to provide the "good life."

What is the "good life" and how does the state provide it? To answer the second question first, the state provides peace and leisure for its citizens, the former by a military and police, the latter by division of labor in supplying the necessities of life. Peace and leisure enable humans to form friendships and voluntary associations, important parts of the "good life." Peace and leisure allow for the pursuit of knowledge. And since humans delight in emotional expression, the larger society of the state allows for participation in cultural events like plays, concerts, art exhibitions, or sports—all part of the "good life."

By calling the state a "creation of nature" Aristotle affirms that man is essentially a social being. Also implied is the further assertion that humans are social in a way that is distinct from other "social animals" like bees and ants who have highly structured societies which serve to get them the necessities of their kind of life. The reason is that human organization is learned, animal organization is only instinctive. Human organization, as learned, is consequently varied, flexible, capable of progress, multi-layered, whereas animal organization has none of those attributes. For example, human societies don't have the same form of government, unlike beehives and anthills. Humans have one man rule, committee rule, parliamentary rule, and the same group can have those different forms at different times. Humans can extend or limit participation in their government. Humans can conduct elections for posts or make appointments for offices. Humans can find more efficient ways of doing things like administering taxes and selecting jurors. Humans have city, state, federal levels of organization, and even multi-national organization. Nothing like that is found in the non-human world. Human social organization in states is different in kind from any kind of ant or bee colony.

FRIENDSHIP

It is a truism that men need and desire friends. And the word "friend" is a word with positive connotations—loyalty, support, love, helpfulness. Aristotle had an analysis of friendship that still holds up today:

The kinds of friendship may perhaps be cleared up if we first come to know the object of love. For not everything seems to be loved but only the lovable, and this is good, pleasant, or useful; but it would seem to be that by which some good or pleasure is produced that is useful, so that it is the good and the pleasant that are lovable as ends. . . .

Now there are three grounds on which people love: of the love of lifeless objects we do not use the word 'friendship'; for it is not mutual love, nor is there a wishing of good to the other (for it would surely be ridiculous to wish wine well; if one wishes anything for it, it is that it may keep, so that one may have it oneself); but to a friend we say we ought to wish what is good for his sake. But to those who thus wish good we ascribe only goodwill, if the wish is not reciprocated; goodwill when it *is* reciprocal being friendship. Or must we add 'when it is recognized'? For many people have goodwill to those whom they have not seen but judge to be good or useful; and one of these might return this feeling. These people seem to bear goodwill to each other; but how could one call them friends when they do not know their mutual feelings? To be friends, then, they must be mutually recognized as bearing goodwill and wishing well to each other for one of the aforesaid reasons.

Now these reasons differ from each other in kind; so therefore, do the corresponding forms of love and friendship. There are, therefore, three kinds of friendship, equal in number to the things that are lovable; for with respect to each there is a mutual and recognized love, and those who love each other wish well to respect in which they love one another. Now those who love each other for their utility do not love each other for themselves but in virtue of some good which they get from each other. So too with those who love for the sake of pleasure; it is not for their character that men love ready-witted people, but because they find them pleasant. Therefore those who love for the sake of utility love for the sake of what is good for *themselves*, and those who love for the sake of pleasure do so for the sake of what is pleasant to *themselves*, and not in so far as the other is the person loved but in so far as he is useful or pleasant. And thus these friendships are only incidental; for it is not as being the man he is that the loved person is loved, but as providing some good or pleasure. Such friendships, then, are easily dissolved, if the parties do not remain like themselves; for if the one party is no longer pleasant or useful the other ceases to love him. . . .

Perfect friendship is the friendship of men who are good, and alike in excellence; for these wish well alike to each other *qua* good, and they are good in themselves. Now those who wish well to their friends for their sake are most truly friends; for they do this by reason of their own nature and not incidentally; therefore their friendship lasts as long as they are good—and excellence is an enduring thing. And each is good without qualification and to his friend, for the good are both good without qualification and useful to each other. So too they are pleasant; for the good are pleasant both without qualification and to each other, since to each his own activities and others like them are pleasurable, and the actions of the good *are* the same or like. And such a friendship is as might be expected lasting since there meet in it all the qualities that friends should have. For all friendship is for the sake of good or of pleasure—good or pleasure either in the abstract or such as will be enjoyed by him who has the friendly feeling—and is based on a certain resemblance; and to a friendship of good men all the qualities we have named belong in virtue of the nature of the friends themselves; for in the case of this kind of friendship the other qualities also are alike in both friends, and that which is good without qualification is also without qualification pleasant, and these are most lovable qualities. Love and friendship therefore are found most and in their best form between such men.

But it is natural that such friendships should be infrequent; for such men are rare. Further, such friendship requires time and familiarity; as the proverb says, men cannot know each other till they have 'eaten salt together'; nor can they admit each other to friendship or be friends till each has been found lovable and been trusted by each. Those who quickly show the marks of friendship to each other wish to be friends, but are not friends unless they both are lovable and know the fact; for a wish for friendship may arise quickly, but friendship does not.[3]

Our first idea of friendship was likely that of a person with whom we could do fun things, like riding a bike, playing a game of cards, or house, or cops and robbers. Friends were playmates. Later, as we learned we enjoyed playing with some and didn't like playing with others, we called only the former friends. No matter how old we get, we like to have friends of that type, even though the things we enjoy may be different, like opera, or books, or college sports, or movies, or gossip. They are probably not the same friends we had in childhood, for their interests and pleasures and ours often change as life moves on.

As we get into the worlds of school and work, we develop new kinds of friends, friends who can help us and whom we can help. Your classmate, John, is good at math, and you are good at English. You do homework together. At the office, you make friends with coworkers who can help you to please the boss, and who can cover for you and you for them, if needs be. Humans form "networks" of friends. You find neighbors with whom you can exchange tools. If you are lucky, you find teachers and mentors who will help you, looking only for the return of your interest and willing efforts. If you are in business, you find it makes sense to know and interact with others in the same business—and this whether you like them or not. In this type of relationship what you can get from it is more important than liking the person. Aristotle called these friendships of utility. These types of friendships are most likely to be or become one-sided; in which case they shouldn't be called friendships at all, for friendship does imply mutuality, give and take.

Almost everybody, sooner or later, has one or two "best friends." "Best friends" are people we can trust, and confide in. They are people who are with us in hard times, like losing a loved one. They have an admiration for us and we admire them, and we value each other for each other's sake. They are helpful and enjoyable to be with, but our relationship isn't built on that, but on love. This friendship Aristotle called "Perfect" or "Complete" since it included the three purposes for friendship—goodness, pleasure, and usefulness. "True friendship" is a name we could give that relationship today. This type of friendship, like all friendships, is a relationship involving mutuality, and goodwill, but it has a depth to it from the trust, unselfish love, and admiration of the goodness of the other that the other types don't usually have.

Thinkers as diverse as Cicero, Francis Bacon, and Ralph Waldo Emerson have written essays on friendship. It is important and valuable for human life, and the loss of friendship is regarded as a significant tragedy. The activity of friendship certainly shows that humans do want to interact with other humans, that we are essentially social beings.

Again, someone might object, we find friendships in the animal world, particularly among domesticated animals, whether of the same kind, or different kinds. However such relationships are only instinctive, while human friendships are chosen. In addition , human friendships are as varied as the purposes and interests of the parties—we have bowling buddies, colleagues at work, shopping companions, business associates, life-long best friends, to name a few. Animals don't confide in one another, or cry on one another's shoulders. A human friend can "double your joys or halve your sorrows." Animals can't do that for one another. Human sociability is essentially a different kind of thing than animal sociability.

VOLUNTARY ASSOCIATIONS

In a society where there is some leisure, human beings look to pursue common interests with others and form groups to do so. Some of the earliest such groups in Greek society were religious guilds. Religious communities of Christian men and women became common from the fourth century and, in Islam, religious communities also developed. With the rise of cathedral schools and universities associations of students and teacher came into existence. In medieval times tradesmen organized themselves into guilds, and devotional societies of all sorts were widespread. In democratic societies, political parties arose.

As leisure has increased and multiplied, so have the opportunities for leisure togetherness with others expanded, exponentially if you will. We have ski clubs, bridge clubs, hiking clubs, garden clubs, bowling leagues and softball leagues. We have fraternal groups like Elks and Moose, Kiwanis, Rotary, Red Cross, Masons, Knights of Columbus, Daughters of Sarah. We have women's groups, men's groups, children's groups. Furthermore, we have labor unions, political action committees, trade associations, and varieties of veterans groups. It is clear we join with other people in things that interest us in some way, like running marathons, or walking for Breast Cancer. It is abundantly clear that such behavior implies that humans are social animals, beings that want to interact with others.

LANGUAGE THE BASIS FOR SOCIABILITY

What makes all the variety and complexity of human relationships and interactions possible is language. Aristotle wrote:

> Now, that man is more of a political animal than bees or any other gregarious animals is evident. Nature, as we often say, makes nothing in vain, and man is the only animal who has the gift of speech. And whereas mere voice is but an indication of pleasure or pain, and is therefore found in other animals (for their nature attains to the perception of pleasure and pain and the intimation of them to one another, and no further), the power of speech is intended to set forth the expedient and inexpedient, and therefore likewise the just and the unjust. And it is a characteristic of man that he alone has any sense of good and evil, of just and unjust, and the like, and the association of living beings who have this sense makes a family and a state.[4]

Aristotle roots the possibility of family and society in the ability of humans to speak, to communicate to one another their needs, to establish an order of fairness to govern their relationships. Husbands and wives need to talk to one another about the division of their labors, about the ways of raising their children. Societies need to be made up of people who communicate about rules for buying and selling and property transfer, laws which protect personal life, family, and property. Humans, Aristotle points out, of all animals, have a sense of right and wrong, and their gift of speech enables them to communicate this to others, and establish societies with justice as their foundation.

In our own time, we frequently read of linguistic feats of animals, particularly chimpanzees.[5] Yet such skills relate to the satisfaction of physical needs, and exhibit nothing like the complexity and diversity of human language. Human language has meaning and grammar, features lacking in animal communication. There are some three thousand human languages, translatable into one another more or less, used for a variety of reasons. No species of animal has multiple languages.

Furthermore, humans speak with others in order to share our feelings, relay information or learn something, give orders or directions, make requests, give consolation, or encouragement, to motivate others, to joke, or relieve tension. We use a different tone of voice or style of writing depending on the purpose of our speaking. We also communicate with others non-verbally too by gestures, touches, facial expressions—some are deliberately chosen, others automatic.

Using language, humans work together, play together, worship together, enjoy plays and books, radio and TV. We have invented instruments like telephones and computers that enable us to engage in conversation with others thousands of miles away. We do enjoy talking to others, and even sometimes weary one another by the non-stop character of our talking. Human language is clearly something different in kind from animal communication.

DENIERS OF HUMAN SOCIABILITY

In the long history of philosophy, only one philosopher has suggested that humans are not naturally social. Thomas Hobbes wrote:

> Whatsoever therefore is consequent to a time of war, where every man is enemy to every man; the same is consequent to the time, wherein men live without other security, than what their own strength, and their

own invention shall furnish with withal. In such condition, there is no place for industry; because the fruit thereof is uncertain: and consequently no culture of the earth; no navigation, nor use of the commodities that may be imported by sea; no commodious building; no instruments of moving, and removing, such things as require much force: no knowledge of the face of the earth; no account of time; no arts; no letters; no society; and which is worst of all, continual fear, and danger of violent death; and the life of man, solitary poor, nasty, brutish, and short.

To this war of every man, against every man, this also is consequent; that nothing can be unjust. The notions of right and wrong, justice and injustice have there no place. Where there is no common power, there is no law: where no law, no injustice. Force and fraud, are in war the two cardinal virtues. Justice, and injustice are none of the faculties neither of the body, nor mind. If they were, they might be in a man that were alone in the world, as well as his senses, and passions. They are qualities, that relate to men in society, not in solitude. It is consequent also to the same condition, that there be no propriety, no dominion, no mine and thine distinct; but only that to be every man's, that he can get: and for so long, as he can keep it. And thus much for the ill condition, which man by mere nature is actually placed in; though with a possibility to come out of it, consisting partly in the passions, partly in his reason.[6]

Hobbes assumes that humans did not always exist with others, that there was a prior "state of nature" in which people existed in isolation from and in competition with one another. Society was invented by humans in order to protect them from each other. Mortimer Adler, a twentieth century thinker, has criticized Hobbes in these terms.

The most important of the modern philosophical mistakes about society is to be found in the theory of the social contract as the conventional origin of the state or civil society. It rests on two myths. One is the myth that goes by the name of "the state of nature." This phrase, when used by Hobbes, Locke, or Rousseau in their slightly varying accounts of the origin of civil society, signifies a condition of human life on earth in which individuals live in isolation from one another and live anarchically with complete autonomy.

What is called a "state of nature" is utterly mythical and never existed on earth. This should be manifest to everyone in the light of the incontrovertible fact that the human species could not have survived without the existence of families for the preservation of infants unable to take care of themselves.

The second myth, inseparable from the first, is the fiction that human beings, dissatisfied with the precariousness and brutality of living in a state of nature, decided to put up with it no longer and to agree upon certain conventions and rules for living together under some form of government that replaced anarchy and eliminated their isolation and autonomy.[7]

Adler also points out that the word "natural" has two meanings. One meaning is by instinct and automatically. The other meaning is "from the nature of the being." It is in this second sense of the word that Aristotle says the state is a "creation of nature" and that humans are naturally "political animals." Intelligence and free choice contribute to the formation of societies, so they do not arise in fixed determined patterns as do those of bees and insects.[8]

Something like the Hobbes' view of human nature was held by the twentieth-century philosopher John Paul Sartre.[9] He describes human love as an attempt to dominate and control the other person. He viewed humans as constantly torturing one another by their interaction, concluding that "Hell is other people."[10] While disagreeing with Sartre about the nature of love, Sartre's contemporary, Gabriel Marcel did note that people often do treat others as objects and not persons.[11] He describes such self-enclosed persons as engaging in *I-It* relationships in which persons are not treated as persons but as functions or objects. However, Marcel points out that humans are capable of deep interpersonal relationships in which they care about the other and are open to his/her needs. In such relationships, called *I-Thou* by Marcel, we treat persons as persons. His description of the *I-Thou* relationship does seem to capture a desire that is part of human nature, a nature that wants interaction with others.

OTHER OBJECTIONS TO SOCIABILITY

Finally, some non-philosophical objections to human sociability ought to be addressed. What about hermits, or misanthropes who want no part of interaction with others? What about those with autism who seem enclosed within themselves? With regard to hermits and people-haters, their isolation is an adult choice to separate themselves from the masses of men and the hurly burley of everyday life, Furthermore, hermits have their books, and religious hermits often have served as spiritual directors or guides to others. Misanthropes have their books, too, and really have their relationships with other people, only they are negative. With regard to the autistic, their un-chosen condition does not mean that humans are not essentially social. For it is more an impairment than a lack of the inclination to interact with others.

REVIEW QUESTIONS

1. Does Aristotle's description of friendship as of three types agree with your experience?
2. What do you think is lacking about Aristotle's view of complete friendship?
3. Do you think that same sex friendships are essentially different from opposite sex friendships?
4. Have you ever spent a waking hour without using language? What does this tell you about your human nature?
5. Does the essential trait of sociability imply that everyone is friendly and outgoing? Are quiet, reserved people really not social by nature?

"MAN AS A PERSON IS NATURALLY SOCIAL"[12]
JOHN PETERS

The Meaning of "Social." Every finite subsistent being by virtue of its essence, properties, activities and passivities, refers to all other beings by relations of agreement and difference, of exercising influence and being influenced. This being-together of beings expresses itself more particularly in the dealings which living beings, and especially sensitive beings, have with their surroundings.

However, just as man because of his spiritual nature is subsistent in an eminent way, so also has he an eminent relationship to the other beings through his intellectual powers of understanding and loving—in a kind of immanence he "is in a way everything."

Above all other relationships which man as a person has naturally, we must place his relations to fellow men who, like him, through their spiritual nature are free persons. Before the level of man is reached, relations are not relations in the full sense. Insofar as man by his very nature is directed to such interhuman relations, we speak of his social nature—the term "social" being derived from the Latin *socius*, companion.

In a degraded sense of "social" one could attribute a certain social instinct to animals insofar as some animals for their self-realization need to live together with others of their species, to which they owe their lives or with which they band together for a shorter or longer time to secure food, security, or reproduction.

Man, who is less self-sufficient than animals, depends more and longer on others of his species. The utilization of the world through technique, labor, and economy is at once collaboration with fellow human beings, and in this collaboration the useful result is increased through specialization and commerce. Although higher cultural life, as it manifests itself in beauty, art, and science, is a matter of eminently personal activity, it too is no less essentially a social affair which runs its course in the interchange of spiritual goods. Language, which alongside the hand and tools is the instrument *par excellence* of human activity, and which because of its signifying function is indispensable for the development of the person even in his most personal thought, is accepted from the forebears, modified, and transmitted to the descendants. Thus from his very birth man lives in a world that is already shaped and named by human beings, he lives in a cultural milieu that is essentially social.

Personal Social Relationships. Man, however, does not only *need* fellow human beings in order to search his own natural good. The proper and primary sense of the social nature of man *as a person* is that man is related to the others *as persons*, as subsistent beings whose self-realization is a purpose in itself and who may not be used by others as *pure* means. Man is naturally orientated to *personal* relationships.

Persons possess a closed subsistence but, precisely because of this, also universal openness: through knowledge they are related to the other in his individual originality without losing themselves. "True" knowledge of fellow men begins by acknowledging that they are persons. It is only when they have been recognized as such that affirmative or negative affective attitudes follow, such as to esteem or despise, to love or to hate, to seek or to flee, to hope or to fear, to bear with or to be angry, to envy or not to envy.

These intellectual and affective attitudes are the foundation of *social acts* in which human beings reciprocally meet and speak to one another about other beings or about themselves in the indicative, optative, or imperative moods, questioning and replying, warning and exhorting, requesting and counseling, begging and commanding, obeying and resisting.

In this social intercourse persons can manifest the sentiments which they have for one another. They are capable of responding to these sentiments in reciprocal affective acts, all of which imply either something of hatred or something of love. When there is mutually expressed affectionateness, a personal bond arises, which can vary from an initial rather general benevolence through all levels of friendship to strictly personal love.

On the basis of social acts and actual affective expressions there may arise more permanent relationships of one human being to another, and if they are reciprocated, also permanent relationships *between* human beings. In some cases the subjects of these relationships have been given special names; for instance, we speak of man and wife, relatives, friends, colleagues, parents and children, teacher and pupil.

Moral Social Obligation. The first moral duty flowing from man's social nature as a person is the recognition that every other human being, no matter who he is, is a fellow man, an "other ego," an intellectual and moral person, at least in capacity and vocation.

This recognition, which implies a certain initial benevolence, has to be maintained and developed in our dealings with our fellow man. It is the foundation of all social virtues, and first of all of justice. The explicitation of this initial benevolence in friendship and love for some human beings with whom we find ourselves connected by special bonds or with whom we freely bind ourselves is the crown and the purpose of the social virtues.

Seen in this light, the self-realization of a being whose mode of *being* is a being-together implies a certain loving dedication to others. For this reason the concrete norms of morality do not explicitly speak of self-love, but of our relationship to fellow human beings. It is only through the practice of faith, hope and charity toward the others, as determined by the bond flowing from the spatio-temporal situation which we have accepted or freely chosen, that man becomes what he should be—more himself by means of a more intimate participation in the mode of *being* of the others.

What has been *ontically* stated regarding the tendency of every being to *self-realization* through activity is, therefore, ethically understood in a more profound sense for man as a person when we say: "A finite personal being becomes more himself according as he enters more in true *communication* with others, by including the true well-being of fellow persons in his own well-being and taking care of it in the same way." Thus we understand better that subsistence and relativity do not exclude but rather include each other.

Person and Society. The fact that man as a person is by nature social has still another meaning—namely, that he is essentially connected with societies, which transcend the individual. The habitual relationships between human beings under certain conditions give rise to objective wholes, each of which presents itself as if it were one being. Relations exist *between* persons, and a society *contains* persons, as its members. By means of analogy with individual persons, the society is the subject of activities, attitudes, and relations. It presents itself, therefore, as an ordered unity of persons, having a quasi-substantial essence and existence, quasi-proper powers, acts and activities.

The question must be raised whether man's being-a-person does not exclude that he can be a means for something else, so that he cannot be a non-subsistent part of a greater subsistent whole. Is his being-a-person not in contradiction with his membership in a society?

The reply is in the negative if one does not conceive the unity of a society as the absolute unity of a single subsistent being, but as the relative unity of many subsistent beings. Although in language and concept we attribute a quasi-subsistence to a society of persons, when we investigate the conditions under which such a quasi-subsistence is possible, we find that the many individual persons are considered precisely insofar as they are together and collaborate in orderly fashion to one and the same purpose. Thus not the society itself is the ultimate subject of powers and acts, but the persons composing it in their mutual relations. If, then, we substantialize society in speech, we merely use a concise form of expression to indicate the many ultimate subjects insofar as their thinking, willing, and acting run their course in connection with the thinking, willing, and acting of the others. The personal pronoun "we" indicates each "I" in its polar reference to the other "I's". The society, therefore, is nowhere else really present than in each of the persons and as a network of relations. However, it is present in each of the members in a different way, according to the place which this member occupies as one of the many poles or terms of the network.

Natural and Free Societies. Two fundamental kinds of society may be distinguished, although concrete societies will usually have something of both types.

First of all, the social relations themselves may be essential for the self-realization of the person. In such a case living-together is sought for its own sake, precisely as living-together, as social communication and mutual enrichment. The purpose of such a society of *life* coincides with the very purpose of each person taken separately. The society aims at making each person attain his natural good in active and passive communication with his fellow men.

Secondly, social relationships may be directed to the attainment of a purpose which for each of the members is a "means" to his personal self-realization. In the production and distribution of these useful means a norm is imposed by the harmony of mutual interests and by the requirements of the *utilitarian* society itself as a quasi-subsistent being, directed to self-preservation and self-development. The production of the useful goods has to be regulated by mutual consent, which is arrived at either in consultation with the interested parties or by following the directives of a few bearers of authority. The possession also of these goods must be divided according to the merits and needs of the members. This coordination limits the individual in his freedom both to produce such goods and to appropriate what is produced or discovered.

By nature man is a member of the all-embracing society of human beings. This society, however, is too vast to act as a unit; the rights which it confers and the duties which it imposes are no others than the above-mentioned moral relations of man to man. The membership of this all-embracing society, therefore, has its intermediary in the membership of societies with smaller numbers, which as particular centers of relations can present themselves to other persons and other societies.

By nature man holds membership in the limited society of the family in which he is born and raised and the nation to which he belongs through descent, language and customs. To reach its welfare, the family needs to live in a broader organization, so that in this sense the family is not a "perfect" society. Hence we may say that man is by his very nature directed also to "civic" societies, such as the village, city, region, state, federation, and commonwealth, which contain more members and therefore make it possible to arrive at greater specialization and a broader satisfaction of needs. However, such societies are less naturally given with human nature itself than are family and nation in this sense that their limits and organizations depend more on the free will of the members, as this will manifests itself in human history. The first, but not the only, task of a civic society is to create a positive order of law.

Finally, marriage is also a natural society in a very fundamental sense. For its essence and purpose lie anchored in the very nature of human beings as man and woman. On the other hand, contrary to the society of the family at least insofar as the children are concerned, every individual marriage bond depends for its origin on the free self-determination of the partners.

Alongside the natural societies, there are also free societies, such as unions, associations, groups, parties, fraternities, etc. While the purpose of the natural societies is determined by human nature itself, that of free organizations is established by positive human decisions. Although it is true that the rise of free societies is in line with man's social nature, nevertheless, the concrete individual free organizations arise only through being freely established by man. The entrance also in an existing free organization is an act of self-determination.

QUESTIONS ABOUT THE PETERS' ARTICLE

1. Cite several ways in which Peters supports ideas already mentioned in this Chapter.
2. What does Peters add to the case for human sociability?
3. What other attributes or essential traits of the human mentioned by Peters, contribute to human sociability?
4. Name one or two words/concepts that Peters uses that require clarification.

NOTES

1. See James Reichmann, S.J. The Philosophy of the Human Person. (Chicago: Loyola Press, 1985). 230-32.
2. Aristotle, *Politics,* Book I. Chapter 1. c. 1-2.1252a—1253b40.
3. Aristotle, *Nicomachean Ethics* Book VIII. c. 3-3 1155b16-1156b32.
4. Aristotle, *Politics* 1251b7ff.
5. See, for instance," Chimpanzee's Use of Sign Language" by Roger and Deborah Fouts in Cavalier, Paola, and Singer, Peter, ed. *The Great Ape Project,* (New York: St. Martin's Press, 1993), 218-41 See also George Johnson "Chimp Talk Debate: Is it Really Language?" *The New York Times,* June 6, 1995.
6. Thomas Hobbes, *Leviathan c. 13.*
7. Reprinted with the permission of Scribner, a Division of Simon and Schuster Adult Publishing Group from *Ten Philosophical Mistakes* by Mortimer J. Adler, ©1985. All rights reserved, 179-180.
8. Adler, *op. cit.,* 172.
9. John Paul Sartre. *Being and Nothingness.* Trans. Hazel Barnes. (New York: Washington Square Press, 1966), 384ff.
10. John Paul Sartre, *No Exit,* the very last sentence.
11. Gabriel Marcel. *Being and Having.* Trans. Katherine Ferrer. (New York: Harper and Row, 1965), 106-107.
12. John Peters, *Metaphysics: A Systematic Survey.* (Pittsburg: Duquesne University Press, 1963), 363-68. Reprinted with permission.

Chapter 3

HUMAN INTELLIGENCE

One of the oldest definitions of a human being is "rational animal."[1] The word "rational" is a synonym for "intelligent." Either word means *"Capable of reasoning, having the ability to grasp relationships and purposes."* The ability to grasp relationships enables humans to develop languages which connect thought and its physical expression; to design skyscrapers and sports stadiums, to invent computers, cell phones and airplanes. Human intelligence allows us to put in place legal systems, financial institutions, schools at multiple levels. Intelligence enables us to develop medical technology, to cultivate the fine arts, to keep history, and to devise games and entertainment of all sorts. It allows us to establish the social organizations that are so much a part of human life. Intelligence enables humans to discover the moral responsibilities that go with being a family member, citizen, or colleague. The ability to grasp relationships is the foundation of every branch of theoretical and practical knowledge, from astrophysics to zoo-keeping.

RATIONALISM

"All men by nature desire to know."[2] In all our waking hours we are ready to grasp reality as it is, or envision it as it could be. However, things are not always the way they seem to be—a mountain looks much closer than it actually is; a berry that looks pleasing may taste bitter; a wall that appears hard may be paper mache. And sometimes our own conditions distort our perceptions, as in sickness when we can't taste or smell well, or when we are impaired by color blindness or deafness to certain pitches. It was considerations such as these that led the first great Western philosopher Plato to mistrust the information delivered by our senses and insist that only our minds can lead to truth. He expresses this concept in his famous Allegory of the Cave.

> Next, said I, compare our nature in respect of education and its lack to such an experience at this. Picture men dwelling in a sort of subterranean cavern with a long entrance open to the light on its entire width. Conceive them as having their legs and necks fettered from childhood, so that they remain in the same spot, able to look forward only, and prevented by the fetters from turning their heads. Picture further the light from a fire burning higher up and at a distance behind them, and between the fire and the prisoners and above them a road along which a low wall has been built, as the exhibitors of puppet shows have partitions before the men themselves, above which they show the puppets.
>
> All that I see, he said.
>
> See also, then, men carrying past the wall implements of all kinds that rise above the wall, and human images and shapes of animals as well, wrought in stone and wood and every material, some of these bearers presumably speaking and others silent.
>
> A strange image you speak of, he said, and strange prisoners.
>
> Like to us, I said. For, to begin with, tell me do you think that these men would have seen anything of themselves or of one another except the shadows cast from the fire on the wall of the cave that fronted them?
>
> How could they, he said, if they were compelled to hold their heads unmoved through life?
>
> And again, would not the same be true of the objects carried past them?
>
> Surely.
>
> If then they were able to talk to one another, do you not think that they would suppose that in naming the things that they saw they were naming the passing objects?
>
> Necessarily.
>
> And if their prison had an echo from the wall opposite them, when one of the passers-by uttered a sound, do you think that they would suppose anything else than the passing shadow to be the speaker?[3]

When Plato says that we are like the prisoners, he is saying that we tend to be deceived by our senses, taking the shadows and reflections of things as if they were reality. Plato is not saying that we actually do confuse the shadow cast by a person with a real person, or the reflection of a tree in a pond with a real tree—even Mr. Magoo would not do that. What he is saying is that the individual persons and objects that we see are not really known if they are known only in terms of their physical attributes, attributes which are constantly changing. Only when we get to the essential unchanging nature of something, do we know it, and that ability is the function of our mind.

Plato also writes:

As long as we have this body, and an evil of that sort is mingled with our souls, we shall never fully gain what we desire; and that is truth. For the body is forever taking up our time with the care which it needs; and, besides, whenever diseases attack it, they hinder us in our pursuit of real being. It fills us with passions, and desires, and fears, and all manner of phantoms, and much foolishness; and so, as the saying goes, in very truth we can never think at all for it. It alone and its desires cause wars and factions and battles; for the origin of all wars is the pursuit of wealth, and we are forced to pursue wealth because we live in slavery to the cares of the body. And therefore, for all these reasons, we have no leisure for philosophy. And last of all, if we ever are free from the body for a time, and then turn to examine some matter, it falls in our way at every step of the inquiry, and causes confusion and trouble and panic, so that we cannot see the truth for it. Verily we have learned that if we are to have any pure knowledge at all, we must be freed from the body; the soul by herself must behold things as they are.[4]

In this quote, with little metaphor, Plato makes clear that it is the soul (the mind or thought) that leads us to truth and that the body is a hindrance to the attainment of truth.

Plato has another literary figure that expresses his viewpoint, the simile of the line.[5] He asks us to image a vertical line divided in two, with two sections to each part. The upper part represents the intelligible world, a world of unchanging objects. The lower part represents the world of sense, a world of changing objects. Genuine knowledge comes when the mind fastens on unchanging objects; opinion, when the senses deal with changing objects. Expressed schematically, this is what we have:

STATES OF MIND		DEGREES OF REALITY
Vision of the Good		The Good
Pure thought, dialectic	**A**	The forms
Reasoning, calculating from premises and with illustrations	**B**	Mathematical entities
Believing, practical activity	**C**	The physical world
Suffering from illusions	**D**	Shadows, reflections

Figure 3.1 States of Mind and Degrees of Reality [6]

For Plato, there are varying degrees of reality, and accordingly various degrees of knowledge. The degree of knowledge given to information discovered by the senses (C and D) is described by Plato as opinion or belief, because it could be wrong, depending as it does on objects that change (C and D). The knowledge furnished by the mind (B and A) is genuine knowledge for its objects never change. For example, we see a tree and it has leaves, the next day it does not have leaves, so our "knowledge" of the tree is only "opinion", if based on sense. The mind's objects (B and A) are called by Plato "Forms" or "Ideas," and they are understandings of meanings, or essential definitions, that exist somehow in a world apart. Unlike individual trees or men, the "Forms" of man or tree do not change with time, or vary from individual to individual. We really know a tree when we know precisely what it is that makes a tree a tree, and we really know a human when we know what essentially constitutes a human, and not just accidental features like hair color, height, or age. The meaning of a tree or a human does not change, and so our understanding of them deserves the name "knowledge."

Plato's view of knowing is known as *rationalism*, and can be defined as *the view of knowledge that holds that only intellectual knowledge, knowledge that is abstract and universal, is reliable, and therefore the senses cannot be trusted.* This view is closely connected with his philosophical view about forms. Looking at it just as a theory about knowing, we can see its strength in upholding the existence of knowledge against skeptics who would deny the existence of knowledge. Plato is also opposing materialistic philosophies which would accept only sense knowledge. However, as Plato's pupil Aristotle pointed out long ago, Plato fails to give the senses their due. Under the proper conditions, they can give us authoritative knowledge of particulars, e.g. this stone is hard; this shirt is white; that flower has a special fragrance; this piece of candy tastes sweet.[7] Furthermore, it is really illogical to doubt the senses because of matters like optical illusions, or conditions within the organism, because we are able to correct mistaken judgments about senses, by reapplying the senses or different senses, as when we feel that the toothpick is not really bent in the glass as it appears to be, or that a hard wall is really soft.

MODERATE REALISM

The critique of Plato's view of knowing was developed by Aristotle into a system called moderate realism. *Moderate realism is the view of knowing that says both sense knowledge and intellectual knowledge are reliable, that knowledge begins with sense knowledge, and that most intellectual knowledge is acquired by a process of abstraction, a process involving both senses and intellect.* Moderate realism also holds that we directly encounter the real world in knowing, and that intellectual knowledge and sense knowledge differ in kind. Aristotle writes:

> Observation of the sense-organs and their employment reveals a distinction between the impassibility of the sensitive faculty and that of the faculty of thought. After strong stimulation of a sense we are less able to exercise it than before, as e.g. in the case of a loud sound we cannot hear easily immediately after, or in the case of a bright colour or a powerful odour we cannot see or smell, but in the case of thought thinking about an object that is highly thinkable renders it more and not less able afterwards to think of objects that are less thinkable: the rea-

son is that while the faculty of sensation is dependent upon the body, thought is separable from it.

Since we can distinguish between a magnitude and what it is to be a magnitude, and between water and what it is to be water, and so in many other cases (though not in all; for in certain cases the thing and its form are identical), flesh and what it is to be flesh are discriminated either by different faculties, or by the same faculty in two different states; for flesh necessarily involves matter and is like what is snub-nosed, a *this* in a *this*. Now it is by means of the sensitive faculty that we discriminate the hot and the cold, i.e. the factors which combined in a certain ratio constitute flesh: the essential character of flesh is apprehended by something different either wholly separate from the sensitive faculty or related to it as a bent line to the same line when it has been straightened out.[8]

Thomas Aquinas, fifteen centuries later, defends moderate realism:

For even in sensible things it is to be observed that the form is otherwise in one sensible than in another: for instance, whiteness may be of great intensity in one, and of a less intensity in another: in one we find whiteness with sweetness, in another without sweetness. In the same way the sensible form is conditioned differently in the thing which is external to the soul, and in the senses which receive the forms of sensible things without receiving matter, such as the color of gold without receiving gold. So also the intellect, according to its own mode, receives under conditions of immateriality and immobility, the species of material and mobile bodies: for the received is in the receiver according to the mode of the receiver. We must conclude, therefore, that through the intellect the soul knows bodies by a knowledge which is immaterial, universal, and necessary. . . .

According to the opinion of Plato, there is no need for an active intellect in order to make things actually intelligible; but perhaps in order to provide intellectual light to the intellect, as will be explained farther on. For Plato supposed that the forms of natural things subsisted apart from matter, and consequently that they are intelligible: since a thing is actually intelligible from the very fact that it is immaterial. And he called such forms *species or ideas*; from a participation of which, he said that even corporeal matter was formed, in order that individuals might be naturally established in their proper genera and species: and that our intellect was formed by such participation in order to have knowledge of the genera and species of things. But since Aristotle did not allow that forms of natural things exist apart from matter, and as forms existing in matter are not actually intelligible; it follows that the natures or forms of the sensible things which we understand are not actually intelligible. Now nothing is reduced from potentiality to act except by something in act; as the senses are made actual by what is actually sensible. We must therefore assign on the part of the intellect some power to make things actually intelligible, by abstraction of the species from material conditions. And such is the necessity for an active intellect.[9]

What is distinctive about this view of moderate realism is its whole-hearted acceptance of the human senses both as vehicles of knowledge themselves and as participants in intellectual knowledge. Aristotle is clearly on the side of common sense, when he affirms the validity of sense knowledge. We are able to see objects in our path and avoid them, feel cold and dress ourselves accordingly, distinguish grapes from stones—all by using our senses.

Aristotle's theory of the origin of knowledge by abstraction was made possible by a radical transformation of Plato's Theory of Forms. Aristotle held that "Forms" or meanings, or natures or essences, were embodied in the things. A tree was a tree because it embodied within itself a "Form" of tree. Water was water because it had the "Form" of water in it. The process of abstraction was a process of discovering the form or nature of the thing embodied in it, a discovery that had to be made by a power other than the senses which delivered the physical details of the object—color, shape, size, smell, sound. *Abstraction is the process of grasping the essential nature of an object, or an aspect of an object.* Every time you learn the meaning of a common noun, like man, woman, child, table, chair, bed, eye, ear, nose, you are abstracting. When you know what a man is, you know that he can be any color, be tall or short, old-looking or not, chubby or thin. When you grasp what a table is, you know a table can be round or square, or rectangular; it can be made of wood, metal, plastic, glass; it can have a variety of colors. When you know what the color red means, you know that it applies to the redness of human hair, of clothing, of fire engines, or nail polish.

The end product of the process of abstraction is called an idea or concept. Ideas have two characteristics: they are abstract, and universal. Abstract means that an idea is without exact details other than those implied in the meaning. For instance, the idea of a square refers to a four equal-sided and right-angled figure. As abstract, it includes the square-ness of a piece of tile on the floor, a piece of candy in a box, a table in the kitchen, a drawing on the board. The idea of a human being is without the important details of sex, age, height, weight, color, nationality, education or whatever.

The other trait of intellectual knowledge, universality, means apply-ing to all things that embody that meaning. Triangle refers to all three-sided closed plane figures regardless of the length of their sides, or whether they are right triangles, acute triangles, isosceles triangles. The idea "car" refers to Fords and Chevys, Fiats and Yugos, Lexuses and Hondas and all brands. In a sense when you know what one car is essen-tially, you know them all.

Our idea of something is not to be confused with our image of it, which is something physical. Images are like proper nouns: they only refer to one specific person, place or thing. By looking at a square win-dow pane, I form an image of glass with definite dimension, embedded in a specific background. By looking at square tile on a floor, I get a spe-cific colored image of a definite dimension and texture. In holding a square piece of candy, I get an image of brown, feel of soft, a smell of sweet, dimension of one inch. Our images are so composed of details, that they can only be specific, individual. And the details make images concrete rather than abstract, and they prevent the image from having a universal reference.

Furthermore, humans are capable of levels of abstraction. Take, for instance, the idea "color". It includes not only the traditional seven, but hundreds of combinations, shades and hues. Yet there is nothing in the real world which is a color, as there is a tree, or a dog. We all know what food is. It includes meat, potatoes, vegetables, pasta, fish, and cake. There is no physical object called food. "Food" is an abstraction. Fur-thermore, we speak of civil rights, moral responsibilities, freedom, free enterprise, though no individual objects perceived by the senses exist corresponding to those names. We are operating on a level of abstraction.

Because we are able to think abstractly, we can connect our thoughts, affirming or denying relationships, as when we say "Circles are round;" "Today is hot;" "Macy's is a good place to shop." Sometimes we deny the relationships of our concepts, as when we say, "Tomorrow is not a holiday;" "Odd numbers are not the same as even numbers;" or "Smok-ing is not conducive to your health." Such an affirmation or denial of the relationships between concepts (and things) is called judgment.

Humans can relate together their judgments to gain new knowledge, and this process is called reasoning. There are many ways of reasoning, and the branch of knowledge called Logic studies them. Philosophers like to use a type of reasoning called syllogistic, in which from the rela-tionship of two concepts to a third, we conclude their relationship to one another. For example we will argue later that "Spiritual things are im-mortal; the human soul is spiritual; the human soul is immortal." We have already argued, at least implicitly, "Manifestation of the desire to be with others is an indication of sociability in humans. The behavior of humans in forming friendships, families, and states manifests a desire to be with others. Therefore, these behaviors indicate sociability in humans." When we act on moral principles, we are reasoning in this way. For instance, "Stealing is wrong; Not putting in a full day's work is stealing. Therefore, not putting in a full day's work is wrong." Or in practical matters, we may reason: "If I want to lose weight I must diet and exercise; I do want to lose weight; Therefore, I will go on a diet and begin a regimen of exercise." "If you want extra credits; you should do extra work. You want extra credits; You do extra work."

The strength of moderate realism is the strength of rationalism, a powerful affirmation of the human ability to know with certainty and to grasp abstract and universal knowledge. Moderate realism has a more complete understanding of human knowledge and human nature than rationalism. Human beings do have senses that deliver accurate knowledge of particular sensible reality and contribute to intellectual knowledge. Human nature, as we will see later, is not just spiritual, but bodily as well. While it is sometimes a hindrance to thought, the human body is still very much part of the human, and not a shell or prison as Plato asserted.

SENSISM

Plato's rationalism and Aristotle and Aquinas's moderate realism both recognize the existence of abstract, universal knowledge, a knowledge developed by a distinct ability or power of humans called mind or intellect. It is precisely these contentions that the eighteenth-century philosopher David Hume denied. He wrote:

> Every one will readily allow that there is a considerable difference between the perceptions of the mind, when a man feels the pain of excessive heat, or the pleasure of moderate warmth, and when he afterwards recalls to his memory this sensation, or anticipates it by his imagination. These faculties may mimic or copy the perceptions of the senses; but they never can entirely reach the force and vivacity of the original sentiment. The utmost we say of them, even when they operate with greatest vigour, is, that they represent their object in so lively a manner, that we could *almost* say we feel or see it: But except the mind be disordered by disease or madness, they never can arrive at such a pitch of

vivacity, as to render these perceptions altogether undistinguishable. All the colours of poetry, however splendid, can never paint natural objects in such a manner as to make the description be taken for a real landskip. The most lively thought is still inferior to the dullest sensation.

Here therefore we may divide all the perceptions of the mind into two classes or species, which are distinguished by their different degrees of force and vivacity. The less forcible and lively are commonly denominated *Thoughts* or *Ideas*. The other species want a name in our language, and in most others; I suppose, because it was not requisite for any, but philosophical purposes, to rank them under a general term or appellation. Let us, therefore, use a little freedom, and call them *Impressions*; employing that word in a sense somewhat different from the usual. By the term *impression*, then, I mean all our more lively perceptions, when we hear, or see, or feel, or love, or hate, or desire, or will. And impressions are distinguished from ideas which are the less lively perceptions, of which we are conscious, when we reflect on any of those sensations or movements above mentioned. . . .

Nothing, at first view, may seem more unbounded than the thought of man, which not only escapes all human power and authority, but is not even restrained within the limits of nature and reality. To form monsters, and join incongruous shapes and appearances, costs the imagination no more trouble than to conceive the most natural and familiar objects. And while the body is confined to one planet, along which it creeps with pain and difficulty; the thought can in an instant transport us into the most distant regions of the universe; or even beyond the universe, into the unbounded chaos, where nature is supposed to lie in total confusion. What never was seen, or heard of, may yet be conceived; nor is any thing beyond the power of thought, except what implies an absolute contradiction.

But though our thought seems to possess this unbounded liberty, we shall find, upon a nearer examination that it is really confined within very narrow limits, and that all this creative power of the mind amounts to no more than the faculty of compounding, transposing, augmenting, or diminishing the materials afforded us by the senses and experience. When we think of a golden mountain, we only join two consistent ideas, *gold,* and *mountain*, with which we were formerly acquainted. A virtuous horse we can conceive; because, from our own feeling, we can conceive virtue; and this we may unite to the figure and shape of a horse, which is an animal familiar to us. In short, all the materials of thinking are derived either from our outward or inward sentiment: the mixture and composition of these belongs alone to the mind and will.

Or, to express myself in philosophical language, all our ideas or more feeble perceptions are copies of our impressions or more lively ones.

To prove this, the two following arguments will, I hope, be sufficient. First, when we analyze our thoughts or ideas, however compounded or sublime, we always find that they resolve themselves into such simple ideas as were copied from a precedent feeling or sentiment. Even those ideas, which, at first view, seem the most wide of this origin, are found, upon a nearer scrutiny, to be derived from it. The idea of God, as meaning an infinitely intelligent, wise, and good Being, arises from reflecting on the operations of our own mind, and augmenting, without limit, those qualities of goodness and wisdom. We may prosecute this enquiry to what length we please; where we shall always find, that every idea which we examine is copied from a similar impression. Those who would assert that this position is not universally true nor without exception, have only one, and that an easy method of refuting it; by producing that idea, which, in their opinion, is not derived from this source. It will then be incumbent on us, if we would maintain our doctrine, to produce the impression, or lively perception, which corresponds to it.[10]

For Hume, then, knowing is just an association of sensations together, and reasoning, a reshuffling of the stored sensations that we have. There is no distinct power of mind distinct from sense. The human has no ability to understand meanings or grasp connections between events. Hume's viewpoint is known as *sensism* and may be defined: *the view that only knowledge originating from an organ of sense, eye, ear, nose, etc., is reliable and that there are no universal abstract ideas*. For Hume, our idea of a human being or a house is a very fuzzy image which is somehow a composite of every human being or house we have seen. For Hume, I don't really know the connection between sweetness in my mouth and the taste of sugar or candy; it is an association I make because of repeated experiences. To that one might say to Hume, "What about the sugar manufacturers and candy makers?" They know they are producing a product that will taste sweet to the palate.

Hume's account of knowledge does not allow for any genuine knowledge at all. Not only philosophy, but science, history, and personal experience are eliminated as pathways to knowledge. That is why Hume's position is not only sensism but skepticism, a total denial of knowledge.

Evidence for Intelligence

Hume has certainly highlighted the importance of sense knowledge, but at a great cost: the loss of a distinctive feature of humans, the ability to think abstractly and reason. Reflection on three human abilities offers evidence for our essential trait of intelligence: 1. the invention/use of language; 2. the invention/use of tools; 3. the capability of laughter and humor.

Language

Henry Koren has this to say of the invention and use of language:

Language consists in the manifestation of thoughts by means of deliberately and arbitrarily chosen symbols. An arbitrary symbol is any material thing, such as a sound, gesture, or mark, which the user selects to replace and designate something other than itself. For instance, of itself the sound "horse" does not indicate anything else than itself. As a sign, however, it stands for the animal known as a "horse." To use such symbols one must understand that a material thing can stand for, and indicate something else with which it has no natural relation. Such an understanding requires knowledge of *signs as signs* and *relationship as relationship*. But no sense power is capable of knowing a sign as a sign and a relation as a relation, because the senses are limited to the concrete and individual, while sign as sign and relation as relation are abstract and universal. Therefore, again, we may conclude that man has a cognitive potency which exceeds the level of the senses and cannot be reduced to them.[11]

Larry Azar complements these observations:

Although the exact number is unknown, it is estimated that there have been between 8,000 and 10,000 different human languages. In Belgium today, for example, Flemish, Dutch, and French are spoken. More amazingly, there are 400 distinct languages in Nigeria; and the language of the African bushman is highly sophisticated; not only is the language very logical, but there are also four levels of intonation. In addition, among Indians (e.g., the Creoles), male-talk differs from female-talk. This creates a burden for the female, who, as mother, must know male-talk in order to teach it to her sons. (Men have no corresponding duty to know female-talk.) The fact that all people have relatively the same brain size and physiology clearly implies that language diversity is neither a biological mutation nor a property found in sub-humans. ...One cannot but wonder how a materialist [sensist] could explain the fact that in Japanese there are 45 different words which mean "I".

From the preceding, we can assert that only humans employ arbitrary or symbolic language, such symbolism being exemplified not only in ordinary discourse but also in scientific nomenclature. In chemistry, we read HC1 + NaC1 → NaC1 + H2O. Symbols are also indispensable to the mathematician.[12]

TOOL MAKING

With regard to the invention and use of tools, Azar has noted:

Although animals do, in fact, use tools, no animal save man *makes* them. The appellation "*homo faber*" [man the maker] is therefore properly descriptive of the human species. Indeed, the French biologist Henri Bergson will go so far as to identify man as a tool maker: "To define our species, we should say perhaps not *homo sapiens* [man the knower], but *homo faber* [man the maker]. In short, intelligence, considered in what seems to be its original feature, is the faculty of manufacturing artificial objects, especially tools to make tools, and of indefinitely varying their manufacture." Observe that Bergson correctly denotes a tool to be an *artificial* object, not a natural one, such as a tree branch. From the preceding, it is clear that the very words architecture, medicine, windmill, computer, gasoline, electric saw, nuclear power plant, etc., etc. imply a human agent. Accordingly, those reductionists who would, in the final analysis, look upon man as a complex mechanism may with profit reflect upon the truism that the machine, in many ways, is one of the most human of contrivances.[13]

HUMOR

With respect to laughter and humor, Reichmann writes:

The human is the only animal that indulges in humor beyond the level of playful, physical gestures, such as we might witness in the play of the puppy or the otter. Indeed, for the human, most calculated humor is a matter of language, and this is certainly true of jokes, where the intent of the communication is to cause others to smile or to laugh. Yet there

clearly is an element of understanding behind the smile, which is indicative of intelligence. We cannot authentically laugh or smile unless
we have first understood something. If someone tells a joke and we find
nothing funny in it, we say that we do not "get the point." Humor is
truly a form of intellectual play. Thus, the clever storyteller or jokester
builds up to a suspenseful moment when understanding occurs sud-
denly and in a wholly unexpected way. It is because we are "caught by
surprise" that we are amused by the recounting, and the inevitable
physiological reaction of the smile or laugh follows. That is why we do
not think that even a very good joke is so funny the second time we
hear it...

In addition to the qualities of intelligence and surprise, humor also involves the grasp of the incongruous. What strikes us as funny involves
the juxtaposition of two notions that we would not normally dream of
associating. Thus the element of surprise derives from this sudden, in-
stantaneous grasp of the incongruous.[14]

Reichmann points out that smiles and laughter indicate that one understands a situation. He sees humor as the grasping of the incongruity of
words, events, expectations. It requires intelligence to grasp the relationship between what might be, what normally is, and what actually is. And
we can add that inventing jokes is even more evidence of intelligence
than appreciating them.

In summary, the invention and use of language, the ability to make
tools and artificial objects, and the capacity for humor are all evidences
that humans do think abstractly and can grasp and understand relationships. Such abilities are not merely matters of assembling and reassem-
bling sensations as Hume argued. Nor is the human invention of calendars and clocks, the division of time into years, months, days, hours,
minutes, and seconds. The invention of money and credit and the whole
world of commerce are further indications of human's ability to grasp
essential meanings and relationships. Intelligence, or rationality, is surely
an essential trait of humans.

THE IMMATERIALITY OF THE HUMAN MIND

In our discussion of abstraction, we noted that process results in a
universal, abstract concept of a physical object. Since material objects
are all individual and concrete, knowing the material object in a way that
is universal and abstract is not a material form of knowing like sensing a

red color, a loud sound, or fragrant odor. Since the things that a being does reveal its nature, the fact that the human mind knows in a non-material way when it abstracts indicates that it is non-material.

Another evidence of the non-material activity of the human intellect is its ability to operate at various levels of abstraction, as we have pointed out earlier. We can grasp what a color or sound is, though there is no such thing as just plain color that we can see, or sound that we can hear. We can grasp what a liquid is, or food, though there is no substance that is just liquid and nothing edible that is just food. Also we know concepts like justice, freedom, happiness, reputation, obligation, which have no physical traits included in their meanings. Since we know what is non-physical, we must have a non-physical power of knowing.

Another feature of our mind that shows its non-material character is its ability to be aware of itself and to think about its own thinking. Such an activity implies a unity not possessed by a material object which is stretched out in space. Unlike sensation, where what is sensed is distinct from and separate from what is sensing—the red apple I see is distinct from my seeing it—the thinker and his thought of himself as aware of the red apple are united, inseparable, in a unity that is not physical, though it is real. Self-awareness and reflection on ourselves are non-material activities, hence our minds must be non-material.

REVIEW QUESTIONS

1. Can you think of some times when you were deceived by your senses? Was it just the senses that were involved?
2. How is naming a first step to understanding for humans?
3. Explain and illustrate the difference between an idea and an image by comparing the idea of a basketball and the image of a basketball, the idea of a gown with the image of a gown.
4. Do you think Hume's analysis of the origin of the idea of God stands up? Explain.
5. How does the fact that humans can translate from one language to another reveal intelligence?
6. Pregnant women are said to have a "nesting instinct." How does the behavior of a woman fixing up a bedroom for a baby, and a robin fixing a nest differ?
7. How do the various uses for humor in our lives show intelligence?
8. Explain how several features of your daily routine reveal that you have intelligence, the ability to think abstractly, reason, and understand relationships?
9. Explain the three main views about human knowledge.
10. Show that the human intellect is non-material.

ON ARTIFICIAL INTELLIGENCE AND COLLEGE PRESIDENTS[15]
PETER KREEFT

Peter: Oh, Socrates, there you are! I need you to help me solve a problem. I decided to take another philosophy course. I guess your argument for liberal arts the other day took hold of me after all. Anyway, the first day of class the professor raised a question nobody in the class could answer, and it really bugs me.

Socrates: What is the problem and why does it bug you, Peter?

Peter: The problem is: what's the difference between human intelligence and computer intelligence—so-called natural and artificial intelligence? The problem bugs me because I think I might go into computers.

Socrates: You might turn yourself into a program, you mean? That's the only thing that goes into computers. The only language they understand.

Peter: I mean I think I've made my career choice. You've gotten me hooked on this new thing, thinking; and I've always been interested in technology; so I thought I could combine the two by going into computers. It's certainly the field of the future economically speaking—I can make my mint—and it's a technology too. It's even a bit like philosophy, isn't it? Or is it? That's my question: what is artificial intelligence, anyway? Do computers think?

Socrates: Your teacher put the question in your laps but not the answer, eh?

Peter: Yes, he must be one of your disciples. A good, hard question, don't you think?

Socrates: Good, yes; hard, no.

Peter: You mean you think it's an easy one to answer?

Socrates: Yes.

Peter: Well? Don't hold me in suspense. And don't give me some unscientific answer about the soul, either. I want an answer I can verify empirically. What can human thinking do that computer thinking can't? Do you think that's an easy question to answer?

Socrates: Yes.

Peter: Well, my teacher doesn't think so. And according to him neither do thousands of other advanced thinkers today. How can that be, if the question is really so easy?

Socrates: Perhaps because they're so advanced that they have left behind and overlooked the most obvious thing of all.

Peter: What? What? Out with it!

Socrates: Artificial intelligence can't do what your natural intelligence just did.

Peter: What's that?

Socrates: What it's still doing. Don't you even know what you're doing? Stop and think for a minute.

Peter: Oh...oh. Asking questions, you mean?

Socrates: Congratulations. You found the hidden treasure.

Peter: But computers can ask questions if you program them to. You can design and program artificial intelligence, to do anything natural intelligence can do.

Socrates: But can it question its programming?

Peter: If you program it to, yes.

Socrates: But it will never question its last programming.

Peter: No.

Socrates: But we do.

Peter: Oh. But that seems such a simple answer, Socrates. There must be something wrong with it.

Socrates: Ask a simple question; get a simple answer.

Peter: I can't refute it. But there seems to be so much evidence—not that we're only computers, but that the brain is exactly like a computer.

Socrates: It is. But as you just pointed out, we are not just our brains. In fact, brains are like computers in that they are instruments needing to be programmed by a person. The programmer departs at death, leaving his brain and the body it directed.

Peter: Couldn't any computer—whether our brain or any other—be programmed by another computer rather than by a person?

Socrates: Yes.

Peter: Then why do we have to speak of "persons" at all? Why not just computers?

Socrates: Because for such a chain of programming, we need a first, unprogrammed programmer that can question its programming and initiate new programs. Someone must push the first domino.

Peter: Sounds like a new argument for the existence of God.

Socrates: The same principle works here as there, anyway: the principle of causality: that you can't give what you don't have, that effects can't exist without adequate causes, that there can't be less in the total cause than in the effect. This principle seems to require a first cause both for nature and for intelligence, natural or artificial.

Peter: I don't know about God. Let's talk about something we know: ourselves.

Socrates: Something *you* know, perhaps. As for me, I find the self a mystery just as I find God a mystery.

Peter: I thought "know thyself" was your thing.

Socrates: It is. And why do you think I'm still at it after so many years?

Peter: Why is it so hard to know yourself, Socrates?

Socrates: Because the self is the knower. How can the subject become its own object? How can the *I* become an *it*? That's why I find God a mystery, too. The human *I* is the image of the divine *I*.

Peter: But cybernetics has done it, Socrates. Now we know how we think. The mysteries are opening up to the light of science.

Socrates: Really? Then please tell me, and end my lifelong quest: what is the *I*?

Peter: Didn't you say the self was the soul? That's what I learned about you in my philosophy course.

Socrates: Yes.

Peter: And the soul was the mind?

Socrates: Not *only* the mind, but the mind is at least the soul's eye, its light.

Peter: All right, let that qualification pass for now. And the mind is the brain. So it follows that the self is the brain. And now we know how the brain works. So we know ourselves by cybernetics.

Socrates: Whoa, there. Too fast. You slipped that last premise in under the table.

Peter: Which?

Socrates: That the mind is the brain.

Peter: What's the difference between mind and brain, then?

Socrates: The mind uses the brain, as a programmer uses a computer. My internal computer is no more me than any of my external computers are. I'm just more intimately hooked up to it.

Peter: This is getting too abstract for me. Can you make the same point more concretely?

Socrates: Hmmm. Perhaps if my simple argument cannot help you, someone else can, someone who can complexify and fudge the issue.

Peter: How could that be? How could we understand the complex more easily than the simple?

Socrates: Simplicity is often the last and hardest thing in the world to attain. Look. Here comes a man who might help us. Let's try him.

Peter: Oh, no, Socrates. That's President Factor, the head of Desperate State University.

Socrates: Excellent. What better place to look for brains than in the head? If anyone should be wise, it is likely to be your philosopher-king.

Peter: College presidents are not philosopher-kings.

Socrates: Oh? What a pity. Nevertheless I shall test his wisdom. What do you call him?

Peter: We call him "Fudge." Fudge Factor. But you should call him Mister President.

Socrates: All right. Excuse me, Mr. President...

Fudge Factor: Eh? What the devil are you?

Socrates: I am a philosopher. What are you?

Factor: I am the president of this university.

Socrates: So you preside over this Desperate State?

Factor: Eh? Preside? Well, sort of. Yes. What can I do for you? Are you some distinguished visitor from the East?

Socrates: In a way. Your student Peter Pragma here was having some difficulty answering his philosophy professor's question about how to distinguish human intelligence from artificial intelligence, and my answers were too simple to convince him. We thought that perhaps you would condescend to help us.

Peter: It was his idea, sir.

Factor: Well, now, I certainly would like to help you if I can, but I'm afraid cybernetics is just not my expertise.

Socrates: Do you mean you don't know the difference between human and computer intelligence?

Factor: That is not my field.

Socrates: That was not my question.

Factor: Huh? What was your question?

Socrates: Do you know how human intelligence is different from computer intelligence?

Factor: Of course.

Socrates: Well, poor Peter here doesn't. So would you do him the great service of sharing your knowledge with him?

Factor: Hmmm...you know, it's quite a coincidence that you should be talking about computers. I'm on my way to a meeting of the Board to decide whether to fully computerize the running of this university. It would save millions, especially in salaries. But there are a few diehards who are jealous of computers, and then there's the problem of the unions, who don't want us to fire anyone. But the bottom line is our finances, which are in a desperate state...

Socrates: Somehow I think I could have guessed that. Excuse me for interrupting, Mr. President, but poor Peter here is still waiting for your answer to his question.

Factor: Eh? What question?

Peter: What is the difference between human intelligence and computer intelligence?

Factor: I told you, that's not my field.

Socrates: Then you don't know?

Factor: I am not employed by this university to go around philosophizing.

Socrates: I see. You mean you are not programmed to respond in that area.

Factor: This is pointless. Good day.

Peter: Socrates, you insulted the president. See, there he goes, off in a huff.

Socrates: I'm sorry, Peter. It seems as if I further confused you instead of helping you.

Peter: How did you do that?

Socrates: Well, I was supposed to help you *distinguish* human from computer intelligence. But here, it seems, we have a fudge factor: a borderline case that makes the distinction much more difficult to see.

Peter: He does seem rather like a computer, doesn't he? Sometimes I wonder whether the whole human race is beginning to evolve into computers.

Socrates: A fascinating question. If computers are becoming more like us and we are becoming more like them...

Peter: You still didn't answer my question.

Socrates: I did, but you didn't like my answer. It was too simple. Should I try a more complex one?

Peter: Are you insulting me?

Socrates: Why do you think that?

Peter: You make it sound as if my mind, too, is like a computer: good at complexities but unable to understand something simple, like the nose on my face.

Socrates: Do you not see that you just answered your own question? You distinguished computer consciousness from human consciousness by complexity versus simplicity. You now have three answers to your question: the ability to question its most recent programming, the ability to initiate a chain of unprogrammed programming and the ability to understand the noncomplex.

Peter: I don't accept any of those answers as adequate.

Socrates: Then we have a fourth answer: the will, the ability to choose. You can even choose to be irrational.

Peter: Oh. I see.

Socrates: And there we have a fifth answer. You see, you understand. Computers merely receive, store, and supply information, like libraries. Would you say the Library of Congress understands anything?

Peter: The people in it do, and the people who wrote the books in it do.

Socrates: And that is your simplest and ultimate distinction between human and computer intelligence. It is the programmers and users of computers that understand, but not the computers.

Peter: Are you against computers, Socrates?

Socrates: Of course not. Am I against brains? But I am against confusion—against personalizing instruments and instrumentalizing persons, which is what is at stake in this philosophical question about human and computer intelligence.

Peter: I hope I see your clear and simple distinction some day, Socrates.

Socrates: So do I. For what doth it profit a man if he gain a whole data bank but lose his own self?

QUESTIONS ON "ON ARTIFICIAL INTELLIGENCE AND COLLEGE PRESIDENTS"

1. Illustrate, by your own examples, three ways that human intelligence and computer intelligence differ.
2. According to Kreeft, do computer intelligence and human intelligence differ in kind? Why or why not?
3. Are computer intelligence and human intelligence analogous or univocal?
4. What does Kreeft mean when he speaks of "personalizing instruments" and "instrumentalizing persons"?

NOTES

1. Aristotle, *Metaphysics* VII, 1036a29.

2. Aristotle, *Ibid.* I, 980b20.

3. Plato, *Republic*, VII, 514a-515d. Hamilton, Edith; The Collected Dialogues including the Letters ©1981. (Princeton University Press, 1989) renewed. Printed by Permission of Princeton University Press.

4. Plato, *Phaedo*, 66a.

5. Plato, *Republic*, VI, 509.

6. Adapted from G. Kreyche, and J. Mann. Edd. *Perspectives on Reality*, (New York: Harcourt Brace and World, 1966), 39.

7. Aristotle, *Metaphysics* 981b 10-11.

8. Aristotle, *De Anima* III 427-29.

9. Thomas Aquinas, *Summa Theologica*. Trans. Dominican Fathers, (New York: Bezniger Brs., 1947). I)I q. 79 a. 3 response; q. 84 a. 1 response.

10. David Hume, An Enquiry Concerning Human Understanding, 9-11

11. Henry Koren, *An Introduction to the Philosophy of Animate Nature*. (St. Louis, B Herder, 1955), 201-02.

12. Larry Azar, *Man, Computer, Ape or Angel?* (Hanover, MA: Christopher Publishing Co, 1985) 303.

13. Azar, *op. cit.*, 303.

14. Reichmann,. *op. cit.*,182.

15. Taken from "*The Best Things in Life*" by Peter Kreeft. Copyright 1984 InterVarsity Christian Fellowship/USA. Used with permission of InterVarsity Press, PO Box 1400, Downers Grove, IL 60515. ivpress.com.

Chapter 4

HUMAN FREEDOM

Human freedom was a motif running through our account of human sociability and human intelligence. We spoke of friendships and voluntary associations, for instance, relationships that people choose to enter. When we spoke of ability of humans to invent tools, tell jokes or devise calendars and enact laws, we implied that those activities were not just instinctual, but the result of both thought and conscious choice.

Choice does seem to be the core concept in freedom. We are free when we can choose to do something or not do something, when we can decide to pick between the options of hamburgers or hot dogs, or working on an assignment or watching a soap opera. *The ability to act or not act, in one way or another,* is called *free will*. The ability to act or not act is often called freedom of exercise; the ability to act one way or another, freedom of specification.[1]

Freedom means being able to originate an act from within ourselves, being self determined, not other determined. Freedom means being "the captain of my soul." We can wear loud satins or dull plaids, if we want. We can criticize, curse, or bless a fellow human being. Being free does mean you are able to do what you desire to do, whether this is good for you or not, and whether it is good for others, or not.

Freedom also has a condition which is inseparably connected with it. Free actions are those that are not forced, controlled, or necessitated in any way. If someone stronger than I am removes me from my seat, and I didn't ask or okay the move, I was not freely leaving my seat. If I am addicted to alcohol, I am not free to limit myself to a couple of drinks. Most definitions of freedom include the condition of non-compulsion, so we can define *freedom as the ability of humans to act on their own power without any form of compulsion.*

THE VOLUNTARY AND THE INVOLUNTARY

Aristotle discusses the nature of free actions and un-free actions which he calls "voluntary" and "involuntary" in his *Nicomachean Ethics*:

> Since excellence is concerned with passions and actions, and on voluntary passions and actions praise and blame are bestowed, on those that are involuntary forgiveness, and sometimes also pity, to distinguish the voluntary and the involuntary is presumably necessary for those who are studying excellence and useful also for legislators with a view to the assigning both of honours and of punishments.
>
> Those things, then, are thought involuntary, which take place under compulsion or owing to ignorance; and that is compulsory of which the moving principle is outside, being a principle in which nothing is contributed by the person who acts or is acted upon, e.g. if he were to be carried somewhere by a wind, or by men who had him in their power.
>
> But with regard to the things that are done from fear of greater evils or for some noble object (e.g. if a tyrant were to order one to do something base, having one's parents and children in his power, and if one did the action they were to be saved, but otherwise would be put to death), it may be debated whether such actions are involuntary or voluntary. Something of the sort happens also with regard to the throwing of goods overboard in a storm; for in the abstract no one throws goods away voluntarily, but on condition of its securing the safety of himself and his crew, any sensible man does so. Such actions, then, are mixed, but are more like voluntary actions; for they are worthy of choice at the time when they are done, and the end of an action is relative to the occasion. Both the terms, then, 'voluntary' and 'involuntary', must be used with reference to the moment of action. Now the man acts voluntarily; for the principle that moves the instrumental parts of the body in such actions is in him, and the things of which the moving principle is in a man himself are in his power to do or not to do. Such actions, therefore, are voluntary, but in the abstract perhaps involuntary; for no one would choose any such act in itself.
>
> For such actions men are sometimes even praised, when they endure something base or painful in return for great and noble objects gained; in the opposite case they area blamed, since to endure the greatest indignities for no noble end or for a trifling end is the mark of an inferior person. On some actions praise indeed is not bestowed, but forgiveness is, when one does what he ought not under pressure which overstrains human nature and which no one could withstand. But some acts, perhaps, we cannot be forced to do, but ought rather to face death after the most fearful sufferings; for the things that forced Euripides' Alcmaeon

to slay his mother seem absurd. It is difficult sometimes to determine what should be chosen at what cost, and what should be endured in return for what gain, and yet more difficult to abide by our decisions; for as a rule what is expected is painful, and what we are forced to do is base, whence praise and blame are bestowed on those who have been compelled or have not.

What sort of acts, then, should be called compulsory? We answer that without qualification actions are so when the cause is in the external circumstances and the agent contributes nothing. But the things that in themselves are involuntary, but now and in return for these gains are worthy of choice, and whose moving principle is in the agent, are in themselves involuntary, but now and in return for these gains voluntary. They are more like voluntary acts; for actions are in the class of particulars, and the particular acts here are voluntary. What sort of things are to be chosen in return for what it is not easy to state; for there are many differences in the particular cases. [2]

Key to the notion of voluntariness is the idea of accomplishing what you do by your own efforts. Knowledge of what you are doing is also central to voluntariness, as is the absence of compulsion. Difficult cases in which one appears to be driven by necessity, as in the case of the sailors who toss cargo overboard in a storm to save the ship, are still "voluntary." A modern example might be that of the small shopkeeper who has to let go of some help because the business will no longer support them. Wishing one did not have to do the deed does not change the fact that one did it voluntarily and is responsible for it.

A consequence of voluntary action is responsibility. Responsibility means that we are held accountable for our actions. Realizing the many factors that impact on human actions, ethicists and legalists speak about greater or lesser responsibility.[3] They point out that fear, passion, e.g. rage and force, can diminish or even take away responsibility. A person who takes another person's life when enraged is considered less responsible than one who premeditated the killing of a person. Society acknowledges that sometimes the young are not sufficiently knowledgeable to enter into a contract and invalidates their consent to marriage or purchases.

The viewpoint on freedom advocated by Aristotle and the majority of philosophers who have followed him is known as *voluntarism* and is defined as: *the doctrine that humans are free, but are limited in their freedom by moral obligations and the necessity of choosing some sort of good*. The voluntarist sees moral obligations as directing, not coercing, behavior. Evidence of its non-coercive nature comes from the human experience that knowing our obligations doesn't force us to do them. We so often fail to do what we think we should do, what is our duty to do, that it is clear to us that obligation only appeals to us to act, it doesn't make us act.

The idea that we must choose good is just the nature of the human will. You cannot desire nothing, or seek to get nothing. You must seek for something that in some way is desirable, something that is good, whether pleasant, useful, or good in itself.[4]

EVIDENCE FOR FREEDOM

What is the evidence for personal freedom? How does it show itself in human life? Our conscious experience testifies to our freedom.[5] When we act freely, we are aware that we are acting freely. As I type these words on the computer, I know no one is forcing my fingers to touch the keys, and I know that my efforts are not the result of an irresistible urge. In simple acts like selecting what clothes to wear for the day, we realize that we are exercising an option, that we are dressing the way we choose, and we are not being forced. If I am planning to travel by air, I go to "Cheap tickets.com" and find the lowest rates. I make a choice based on price, convenience, and airline, and know I am doing it freely.

We also experience our freedom directly, when we do things that we don't particularly want to do. We reluctantly head for the library as our friends are heading out to party; we visit an elderly relative who doesn't really recognize us all the time; we forego a dessert, because we are on a diet. In fact, a considerable portion of our voluntary action consists in our doing tasks we don't want to do, such as doing and correcting papers in school, keeping our premises clean, and dealing with troublesome people.

In all of our choices, humans have reasons for what they do, or don't do. Such reasons are called motives. They give us a goal to pursue, finishing a chapter, looking good, getting a good deal on an air trip. Motives invite us to act, sometimes incite us to act. However, our motives do not compel us to act. We can leave the computer and make a phone call. We can wear yesterday's clothes if we want. We can cancel the trip, or decide to go by car or train. We can decide to forget about our diet. Of course, when we choose these alternatives, we are acting for a motive, a reason we have decided to follow.

Returning to our experience of our own freedom, we also have what can be called an indirect awareness of our freedom.[6] Before we act, we think over the possibilities for acting, or weigh the pros and cons of an action. Such thinking over possibilities or evaluating the alternatives is called deliberation. If I am booking a flight, I have to decide if price is more important than schedule, or an alternative airport will work without inconveniencing anyone too much. If you are going for a job interview, you have to pick out something that will make you look both attractive and professional. If it is time to register for next semester, you have to decide whether to take a requirement early in the morning or late in the afternoon. In deliberating, we are aware that we do have a choice, that we are free to pick what it is that we want, or are willing to accept. Aristotle has this to say about deliberation:

> We deliberate about things that are in our power and can be done; and these are in fact what is left. . . . Now every class of men deliberates about the things that can be done by their own efforts. And in the case of exact and self-contained sciences there is no deliberation, e.g. about the letters of the alphabet (for we have no doubt how they should be written); but the things that are brought about by our own efforts, but not always in the same way, are the things about which we deliberate, e.g. questions of medical treatment or of money-making. . . Deliberation is concerned with things that happen in a certain way for the most part, but in which the event is obscure, and with things in which it is indeterminate. We call in others to aid us in deliberation on important questions, distrusting ourselves as not being equal to deciding.[7]

Aristotle's main point is that we only deliberate about things possible for us to do. I don't deliberate whether I shall run a four-minute mile, but do deliberate whether I shall walk for two or three miles. I don't deliberate about speaking Russian, but do deliberate about what words to say to a grieving person. Deliberation, then, shows indirectly that I am aware of my freedom, because it involves thinking over possibilities for action, possibilities I know that I have the ability to fulfill.

We also experience our freedom indirectly, when we look back at what we have done and praise or blame ourselves for it. We are pleased if staying in to study rather than going out to party has got us an A on a test. We look back at something we said in anger and regret it; we blame ourselves for not being honest with a friend. This kind of self-judgment implies we know that we could have done differently, that we were not forced to act as we did. The religious practice of examination of conscience, and the educational and business practice of assessment of outcomes are actions that embody an indirect awareness of our freedom, for evaluation of past performances makes sense only on the presupposition something could have been done about them. Evaluation of the past also presupposes the awareness that we can in the future do things differently, if we want to do so—we are not constrained to repeat past mistakes.

LIMITATIONS OF FREEDOM

In being aware that we are free, we also are aware that our freedom has limitations. Every decision we make eliminates a possible choice—by studying, I eliminate going out at that time; by wearing a blue shirt, I eliminate wearing a yellow one at that time; by choosing one person for my spouse, I eliminate all others at the moment of choice. Furthermore, we have physical limitations—we can't leap tall buildings in a single bound. We have financial limitations—I can't give millions to the poor, even if I want to. We have time and space limitations—I can't be in two places at the same time, or book 25 one-hour appointments in a 24-hour day. Also, as we have noted earlier, we have responsibilities and obligations that limit our freedom. A promise to meet a friend for lunch commits us, and does not leave us with the freedom we would have had, if we had not made the promise.

Another limitation on human freedoms comes from the connection between means and ends. Wanting certain goals means you must choose certain actions, although your act of choosing these means is free. If you desire to graduate, you must take required courses. If you want to travel to Europe or Australia from the United States, you must cross water. If you want to be warm in the winter, you must dress warmly and heat your residence.

ANOTHER ARGUMENT FOR FREEDOM

In addition to the experiential argument, which, in a way, is an appeal to the self-evidence of human freedom, philosophers have suggested another argument for free will: the ethical argument. Thomas Aquinas outlined this argument almost in passing back in the thirteenth century: "Man has free will; otherwise, counsels, exhortations, commands, prohibitions, rewards and punishments would be in vain."[8] In other words, what is the point of advising a friend about a job offer, giving a pep talk to a team, if the listeners are not free and their responses will be pro-grammed and un-free. Likewise, the ideas of command and obedience to command presuppose freedom. Making murder and theft illegal would be in vain, if humans were not free, because they would not be able to refrain from those things of their own choice. Finally, how would the notion of reward for something well done, and punishment for evil, be at all effective, if people were not free? Why have a grading system in schools, or bonuses at work, or fines for speeding, and jail for illegal drug use, if humans are making their choices based on something other than their own free will?

DENIERS OF FREE WILL

Among early deniers of free will were the Stoic philosophers who viewed the universe as God.[9] Consequently, the universe was a rational place, and everything in it unfolded according to a rational plan. They developed an ethical system which stressed living according to nature, but the implicit freedom involved in ethics does not fit comfortably with their overall view of cosmic determinism.

Determinism is the word that has come to be used to refer to the view of those who deny the existence of free will. It can be defined: *the view that humans are not free but are necessitated in their actions by forces outside them, inside them, or a combination of each.* In the twentieth century, three varieties of determinism have emerged from scientists immersed in Psychology and Biology. Each operates out of a materialis-tic base, that is, sees humans as only physical. Yet each develops his views from this own work.

FREUD'S PSYCHOLOGICAL DETERMINISM

Sigmund Freud formulated a theory of human consciousness as threefold—an Id, a drive for pleasure; an Ego, a rational power; and a Super-Ego, a "conscience-like" mechanism that is the seat of all the do's and don'ts we have ever heard.[10] Human behavior is then the outcome of three interacting forces and not a free choice. Freud's view is known as *psychological determinism* and may be defined as: *the view that humans are not free but are necessitated by the psychic forces within them such as past experiences and repressed memories.*

Apart from his technical terms, Freud's description of the decision process does seem to describe the struggle that does go on in some of our decisions. For instance, a young man, call him George, is attracted to a young woman and would like to get to know her better, and thinks about asking her to lunch with him. Since the girl is very attractive and has a number of others pursuing her, he wonders whether he has a realistic hope. Also, he has been seeing a girl for a couple of months and feels a loyalty there. George is certainly being pulled, if you will, in different directions. Or take Susan, who has just graduated from college and is offered a job in St. Louis, eight hundred miles from where she has always called home. The pay is good, and the opportunities for advancement are good. However, Susan is very attached to her family, and her parents are beginning to develop some health problems. Also, she has just begun dating a man in the area she is presently living in, and she really likes him. Again, desire, reality, and conscience are pulling in different directions.

If George decides not to ask the girl out, can we say that he was forced to do so, by his conscience, or his fear of being rejected? Is it not rather that George decided that loyalty was more important than physical desire. His behavior was not a resultant of physical forces, or a push by the most powerful motive, but a choice he made to let loyalty be the criterion of his behavior. The fear of rejection may have influenced his behavior, as did his conscience, but they didn't force it. And if Susan takes the job in St. Louis, it will be because she decided to get on her career track early, and realized that she could still be available to her parents while living away, and that romance would come in due time. It wasn't the weight of the career motive that pushed Susan to take the job, it was that Susan chose to give that motive its weight in her decision-making process.

Another observation about Freud's analysis: life is not always a pressure cooker. Every day we make a lot of "no brainer" decisions. My car is low on gas, I go fill it up; it is cold, I put on a sweater; it's raining, so I don't walk outside but use the treadmill; there is ham and turkey in the refrigerator, so I decide to eat ham because I haven't had it in a while. Looking for subconscious causes, repressed feelings, or parental training to explain such behavior is reaching to save a theory at every cost. It is much simpler to accept the fact that we are free beings and exercise this freedom most of the time.

SKINNER'S BEHAVIORISM

Another psychologist of the twentieth century, B.F. Skinner, argues that humans are not free, but are conditioned by their upbringing, and culture, trained to behave much like pets by positive and negative reinforcement of behavior patterns.[11] This viewpoint is often called *cultural* or *psychosocial determinism* and is: *the view that humans are not free but are necessitated in acting by their upbringing, social customs, and even their physical environment.*

Skinner writes:

Man's struggle for freedom is not due to a will to be free, but to certain behavioral processes characteristic of the human organism, the chief effect of which is the avoidance of or escape from so-called "aversive" features of the environment. . . .

Two features of autonomous man are particularly troublesome. In the traditional view, a person is free. He is autonomous in the sense that his behavior is uncaused. He can therefore be held responsible for what he does and justly punished if he offends. That view, together with its associated practices, must be re-examined when a scientific analysis reveals unsuspected controlling relations between behavior and environment.

A much more important role is played by behavior which weakens harmful stimuli in another way. It is not acquired in the form of conditioned reflexes, but as the product of a different process called operant conditioning. When a bit of behavior is followed by a certain kind of consequence, it is more likely to occur again, and a consequence having this effect is called a reinforcer. Food, for example, is a reinforcer to a hungry organism; anything the organism does that is followed by the receipt of food is more likely to be done again whenever the organism is hungry. Some stimuli are called negative reinforcers; any response which reduces the intensity of such a stimulus—or ends it—is more likely to be emitted when the stimulus recurs. Thus, if a person escapes from a hot sun when he moves under cover, he is more likely to move under cover when the sun is again hot. The reduction in temperature reinforces the behavior it is "contingent upon"—that is, the behavior it follows. Operant conditioning also occurs when a person simply avoids a hot sun—when, roughly speaking, he escapes from the *threat* of a hot sun. . . .

Escape and avoidance play a much more important role in the struggle for freedom when the aversive conditions are generated by other people. Other people can be aversive without, so to speak, trying: they can be rude, dangerous, contagious, or annoying, and one escapes from them or avoids them accordingly. They must also be "intentionally" aversive—that is, they may treat other people aversively because of what follows. Thus, a slave driver induces a slave to work by whipping him when he stops; by resuming work the slave escapes from the whipping (and incidentally reinforces the slave driver's behavior in using the whip). A parent nags a child until the child performs a task; by performing the task the child escapes nagging (and reinforces the parent's behavior).... A teacher threatens corporal punishment or failure until his students pay attention; by paying attention the students escape from the threat of punishment (and reinforce the teacher for threatening it). In one form or another intentional aversive control is the pattern of most social coordination—in ethics, religion, government, economics, education, psychotherapy, and family life. [12]

Let us examine the cases of George and Susa in the light of Skinner's views. The facts are the same; however, what made George decide the way he did was his family's stress on loyalty, and the culture's view that dating should be serial, one person at a time. George couldn't help but make that decision not to ask the lovely girl out. Likewise, Susan had to decide as she did, because society programs women to put career first and to live independently. The influence of society is even more evident, if we consider George and Susan as living in another country. Susan more than likely would not have moved, if she lived in India. George would not have been so inhibited, if he were living in France or Italy.

A first response to Skinner might be, "How do you explain the people who call society to task for its injustice, people like Gandhi, Dr. Martin Luther King, Jr.? How do you explain revolutions, political, social, religious, and economic? Inventiveness and novelty cannot be programmed into anyone, or any society. How do you train someone to build computers, if computers don't exist yet? How do minorities ever get their rights recognized, if society dictates behavior?

Let's look at George and Susan from the voluntarist point of view. George's decision is influenced by the customs of young people his age in regard to dating, and by his upbringing, but is it determined, i.e. controlled, by them? George can decide to go against social custom and ask the girl out. If he doesn't ask her out, it is because he chooses to follow the prevailing customs, or to be loyal. Likewise, Susan could decide to turn down the job, either to be near her parents, or near a possible romantic interest. And if she takes the job, it isn't because society has forced her to do so, but because she chose to do so.

Realistically, our upbringing and culture do exert an enormous influence upon our choices. Society limits the number of our options and points us in certain directions. If our society doesn't have airplanes, we can't fly, and if we grow up in the country, we won't be able to play little league baseball. If we do not have a college degree, there are many employers who won't look at us. Furthermore, the benefits or disadvantages that society proposes to us in a legal system do direct a good deal of our behavior, but they do not control it. We can decide it is worth the fine to get a good parking place, or choose to eat unhealthy because it tastes good.

BIOLOGICAL DETERMINISM

A third type of determinism is *biological, genetic, or socio-biological determinism: the view that humans are not free but are necessitated in their actions by their genetic make-up or bodily chemistry.* "Biology is Destiny" is an expression of this stance. If I decide to become a doctor, the desire to do so is prompted by a gene, and so is my choice. If I deal drugs, it is because of physiology. If I marry, it is a choice literally based on "chemistry." E.O. Wilson, coming out of a biological background, is among the most recent exponents of this form of determinism.

> If biology is destiny, as Freud once told us, what becomes of free will? It is tempting to think that deep within the brain lives a soul, a free agent that takes account of the body's experience but travels around the cranium on its own accord, reflecting, planning, and pulling the levers of the neuromotor machinery. The great paradox of determinism and free will, which has held the attention of the wisest of philosophers and psychologists for generations, can be phrased in more biological terms as follows: if our genes are inherited and our environment is a train of physical events set in motion before we were born, how can there be a truly independent agent within the brain? The agent itself is created by the interaction of the genes and the environment. It would appear that our freedom is only a self-delusion.

> In fact, this may be so. It is a defensible philosophical position that at least some events above the atomic level are predictable....

> Most significantly of all, schemata within the brain could serve as the physical basis of will. An organism can be guided in its actions by a feedback loop: a sequence of messages from the sense organs to the

brain schemata back to the sense organs and on around again until the schemata "satisfy" themselves that the correct action has been completed. The mind could be a republic of such schemata, programmed to compete among themselves for control of the decision centers, individually waxing or waning in power in response to the relative urgency of the physiological needs of the body being signaled to the conscious mind through the brain stem and midbrain. Will might be the outcome of the competition, requiring the action of neither a "little man" nor any other external agent. There is no proof that the mind works in just this way. For the moment, suffice it to note that the basic mechanisms do exist; feedback loops, for example, control most of our automatic behavior. It is entirely possible that the will—the soul, if you wish— emerged through the evolution of physiological mechanisms. But, clearly, such mechanisms are far more complex than anything else on earth. . . .

Genetic determination narrows the avenue along which further cultural evolution will occur. There is no way at present to guess how far that evolution will proceed. But its past course can be more deeply interpreted and perhaps, with luck and skill, its approximate future direction can be charted. The psychology of individuals will form a key part of this analysis. Despite the imposing holistic traditions of Durkheim in sociology and Radcliffe-Brown in anthropology, cultures are not superorganisms that evolve by their own dynamics. Rather, cultural change is the statistical product of the separate behavioral responses of large numbers of human beings who cope as best they can with social existence.[13]

Although he uses the language of "maybe", Wilson is denying free will. He offers as evidence only the fact that some behaviors besides atomic behaviors are predictable, and offers the hope that someday science may know exactly how neural connections determine behavior. However, experience shows us that people like George and Susan, although somewhat predictable to those who know them, can act out of character and in a way their friends would never envisage. Likewise the suggestion that the future will show us how we are not free is no evidence for our present lack of freedom—it is the fallacy of the appeal to the future.

A specific example of how biological determinism started to play out in our society is described by Suzuki and Knudson in their book *Genethics*.[14] Researchers found that some men's sexual chromosome had two Y components and were XYY. This discovery, based on analysis of DNA in prisoners, showed many of them with that chromosome to be violent.

Some inferred a causal connection, and suggested infants be screened for that chromosome.

David Suzuki had this critique of genetic determinism:

> The vast majority of human hereditary differences are polygenic, or involving the interplay of many genes; therefore, it is a dangerous simplification to proclaim a causal relationship between human behavior and so called "defects" in human DNA.[15]

The idea that bodily dispositions affect human behavior is not new. The ancients, following the physician Galen, viewed humans as having four temperaments: sanguine, melancholy, irascible, and phlegmatic, depending on the presence of certain humors (liquids) in the body.[16] It is long been noticed that even among infants, some are more active than others. However, human physiology, as we have argued, predisposes to behavior, but does not normally channel it in a specific direction. I may be energetic, but I decide whether my energy will go into working out, cleaning, or a hobby like woodworking. Physical attraction plays a part in many human relationships, as we have seen in our examples of George and Susan. But we know from our own experience and that of others, that George doesn't *have to* ask the girl out, and Susan doesn't *have to* turn down the good job in order to be near a person she is attracted to. In fact, one of the clear indicators that humans differ from animals is in their ability to manage their sexual urges, and to postpone gratification of them to another time, or deny them gratification at all, as celibates have done for ages, and faithful spouses separated from partners have also done.

To sum up our evaluation of determinism: factors like our past experiences imbedded in our psyches, our social environment of friends and family, our bodily state, all of these have an influence on our choices, but they do not control, force, or necessitate them. The extent of their influence is not so much a function of their intrinsic force, as it is our willingness to let these factors give weight to our decisions. The reasons we have for acting are not efficient causes producing our actions, but final causes inviting us to act. The Franciscan philosopher Duns Scotus expressed the nature of free will when he stated: "Nothing is the cause of the volition of the will except the will itself."[17]

EXAGGERATED VOLUNTARISM

The French philosopher John Paul Sartre, whose views on sociability we discussed in Chapter 2, advocated a concept of freedom that is absolute. His view is called *extreme or exaggerated voluntarism*. It is defined: *the view that humans are totally free and not subject to moral obligations.* Sartre rejects the idea of any constraints at all, not allowing that there is any fixed essence that is human nature. He sees a preexisting moral obligation as a destroyer of human freedom, which he champions. One choice is as good as another. "It is the same thing whether one gets drunk alone, or is a leader of nations."[18] He writes:

> Man is free because he is not himself but presence to himself. The being which is what it is can not be free. Freedom is precisely the nothingness which is made-to-be at the heart of man and which forces human-reality to make itself instead of to be. As we have seen, for human reality, to be is to choose oneself; nothing comes to it either from the outside or from within which it can receive or accept. Without any help whatsoever, it is entirely abandoned to the intolerable necessity of making itself be—down to the slightest detail. It will be well therefore to examine the other aspect of freedom, its "reverse side:" its relation to facticity. . . .
>
> It is the same upon the plane of morality. There is this in common between art and morality, that in both we have to do with creation and invention. We cannot decide *a priori* what it is that should be done. I think it was made sufficiently clear to you in the case of that student who came to see me, that to whatever ethical system he might appeal, the Kantian or any other, he could find no sort of guidance whatever; he was obliged to invent the law for himself. Certainly we cannot say that this man, in choosing to remain with his mother—that is, in taking sentiment, personal devotion and concrete charity as his moral foundations—would be making an irresponsible choice, nor could we do so if he preferred the sacrifice of going away to England. Man makes himself; he is not found ready-made; he makes himself by the choice of his morality, and he cannot but choose a morality, such is the pressure of circumstances upon him. We define man only in relation to his commitments; it is therefore absurd to reproach us for irresponsibility in our choice. . . .
>
> Thus, although the content of morality is variable, a certain form of this morality is universal. Kant declared that freedom is a will both to itself and to the freedom of others. Agreed; but he thinks that the formal and the universal suffice for the constitution of a morality. We think, on the

contrary, that principles that are too abstract break down when we come to defining action. To take once again the case of that student; by what authority, in the name of what golden rule of morality, do you think he could have decided, in perfect peace of mind, either to abandon his mother or to remain with her? There are no means of judging. The content is always concrete, and therefore unpredictable; it has always to be invented.[19]

Sartre's claim that we make our being by our choices cannot be literally true—we must exist in order to act. More significantly, there are *a priori* principles that can guide our choices—that we do not take what is another's as our own, for instance, or that we do not betray our friends, or perpetrate sexual violence on another. And if one is a parent, there are *a priori* rules to oblige you, to feed your child, to clothe him, and to protect him. Sartre has falsely inferred from the indeterminateness of positive responsibilities—what food do we feed the child? how do we protect him/her from cold? to the absence of definite obligations.

When challenged that his views amounted to anarchy and were anti-human, Sartre wrote a piece in which he defended his views as humanistic.[20] He agrees that there is a human condition: we live in society and need to get along, speak the truth to one another, cooperate and work for freedom. This "human condition" seems to bring in the back door a "human nature" that he has thrown out the front. For all his bravado, Sartre seems to be saying no more than this: "Every human has a free will and he/she is not compelled by anything to use it wisely, or to choose some more-defined moral good." In other words, it appears that Sartre's position or positions are only reconcilable, if they collapse into the viewpoint of voluntarism.[21]

THE IMMATERIALITY OF THE WILL

Implicit in our arguments for free will has been the idea that free will in humans is not something physical, but spiritual. We have spoken of the fact that humans choose to do unattractive yet valuable things, like changing diapers, or working long hours to support a family, or resisting an urge to eat food that is unhealthy for us, or enter a relationship which would be wrong. In self-denial, in trading "pain" for "gain", we are opting for a higher good, choosing some non-physical goal like care for another, health, morality. Furthermore, we humans have desires and pursue goals which are not physical. We seek a successful career, we want to be respected and admired by our peers. We want to feel loved and to be secure in our present and in our future. Desires for success, good friends, peace of mind and respect from others are not desires for physical things, and so must come from something non-physical that originates our desires and actions, our will.

LOVE

The human will is not just a chooser, it is a lover. Humans have the ability to love, and they do love one another in various ways. The word "love" brings to mind attraction, emotional attachment, affection, all of which are primarily physical, and really not under our control. The physical beauty of another person attracts us; long-time association with family builds bonds of affection; receiving tokens of love from others makes us feel loved. But love also means caring for, committing to and desiring good for another—which are free acts. All friendships involve a mutual good will, something that is chosen. To say "I love you" to another is not just to reveal a feeling, but to make a commitment. To care for a sick child or an elderly parent is a spiritual act, perhaps sometimes prompted by feelings of compassion, but in the long run an outcome and expression of choice. Certainly, love for one's enemies, a value taught by Jesus, is not something that automatically happens; it must be willed. The loves for country, world peace, humans as a whole are loves that are an expression of choice, even if they may have strong emotional, unchosen, components as well.

Love can be directed toward persons, or animals, or even of things. Such love can be concerned primarily with the well-being of the object of love. Such a love is called *love of benevolence: love of another for his/her own sake.* We can also love others for our own benefit, and such a love is called *love of concupiscence: love of another for your own sake.*

Love can be one sided, either because the other can't reciprocate, doesn't realize that he or she is loved; or won't return the love. Love can be reciprocal as in friendship, romantic love, family love, brotherly love. Love can be shared: as two parents who care about their children; or brothers and sisters who care for one another; or a squad of soldiers who are devoted to one another.

The English writer C.S. Lewis states that there are four kinds of love: erotic or romantic love, love of affection, love of friendship, and agapeistic, or self-sacrificing love.[22] The first two are physical and largely un-free. The last two are chosen and free.

The many uses of the word love, the many types of love, indicate that love is an analogous term, a word used with related meanings, but not used in exactly the same way each time. All love is desire for some sort of good. However, as we have seen, desires can be un-free, as in physical attractions, reactions, and attachments, or free as in friendship commitments to justice, country, or God.

REVIEW QUESTIONS

1. Explain and evaluate the argument for free will from experience.
2. Explain and evaluate the ethical argument for free will.
3. Explain and illustrate the difference between "influencing" and "determining/controlling."
4. How is it impossible for a determinist to defend his position coherently?
5. Do you agree with Sartre that laws and moral rules destroy your freedom?
6. Contrast humans and animals in regard to freedom.
7. Explain how motives are final causes of action for voluntarists, efficient causes of action for psychological determinists.
8. Prove that the human will is non-material.
9. Are there any limitations upon human freedom? Explain.
10. Explain how love is analogous.

FREEDOM OF CHOICE[23]
MORTIMER ADLER

This natural freedom is the freedom of the will in its acts of choice. Freedom of choice consists in always being able to choose otherwise, no matter what one has chosen in any particular instance. As contrasted with a freedom that consists in being able to do as one wishes, it might be described as freedom to will as one wishes.

When we declare that freedom is a natural human right we must have in mind the two circumstantial freedoms—the freedom to do as one pleases (within the circumscription of just laws) and the political liberty that comes with citizenship and suffrage. There is no meaning to the statement that one has a right to moral liberty, which can be possessed only with acquired virtue and wisdom; or a right to freedom of choice which, if it exists, is a natural endowment possessed by all.

However, unless freedom of choice does exist, it is difficult to understand the basis of our right to these other freedoms. If we do not have freedom of choice, what reason can be given for our right to do as we please or to exercise a voice in our own government?

These considerations, and there are others to which we will subsequently come, make the controversy about the existence of freedom of choice one with far-reaching consequences....

With knowledge of all the ins and outs of the controversy, I cannot show that the exponents of free choice are right and that the determinists who oppose free choice are wrong. The philosophical defect here is not so much a demonstrable philosophical error as a manifest misunderstanding of the issue itself.

That misunderstanding lies mainly on the side of the modern philosophers and scientist s who are determinists. What I am saying here is not that their denial of freedom of choice is a demonstrable mistake, but rather that they do not correctly understand what they have denied—the premises upon which an affirmation of freedom of choice rests.

Prior to the end of the nineteenth century, determinists held that all the phenomena of nature are governed by causal laws through the operation of which effects are necessitated by their causes. Nothing happens by chance, in that sense of the term which regards a chance event as something uncaused. In their view, an intrinsically unpredictable free choice is exactly like a chance event and so cannot occur within the natural domain. While it is true that a free choice and a chance event are both unpredictable with certitude and precision, it is not true that both are un-caused.

Beginning at the end of the nineteenth century and becoming more significant in our own time, science added statistical laws or probabilistic formulations to causal laws, and in doing so introduced aspects of inde-terminacy into the realm of natural phenomena.

Such indeterminacy, however, does not reduce to the causelessness of chance. A handful of philosophers and Nobel Prize winning scientists advanced the supposition that such indeterminacy might make room for freedom of choice within the bounds of nature; but more sober minds rightly dismissed the supposition. The causal indeterminacy involved in certain scientific formulations, especially those of quantum mechanics, simply bears no resemblance to the causal indeterminacy involved in freedom of choice.

What the determinists who deny freedom of choice on the grounds stated above fail to understand is that the exponents of free choice place the action of the will outside the domain of the physical phenomena stud-ied by science. If their theory of freedom of choice conceived it as a physical event in the same way that the action of our senses and the mo-tion of our passions are physical events, then they would have to accept the arguments of the determinists as adequate grounds for denying free choice.

But that is not the case. The will, as they conceive it, is an intellec-tual, not a sensuous, appetite or faculty of desire and decision. In their view, the human mind, consisting of both intellect and will, is to be sharply distinguished from the senses, the memory, the imagination, and the passions. The latter may operate according to the same principles and laws that govern all the other phenomena of the physical world, but the intellect and the will, being immaterial, do not act in accordance with these principles and laws. They are governed by laws of their own.

The acts of the intellect are either necessitated or they are arbitrary. They are necessitated when they are acts of genuine knowledge, for the intellect cannot say no to a self-evident truth, nor can it say no to any proposition that is supported by evidence and reasons that put it beyond a reasonable doubt or give it predominance over all contrary opinions.

In the above cases, all the intellect's judgments are necessitated. Only when it is confronted with mere opinions, unsupported by evidence and reasons, is its judgment arbitrary—an act of the intellect moved by a free choice on the part of the will rather than an act of the intellect moved by the truth laid before it. In neither case is the action of the intel-lect uncaused or a chance event.

Like the acts of the intellect, some acts of the will are necessitated and some involve freedom of choice. The only object that necessitates the will is the complete or total good. In the presence of the complete or total good, it cannot turn away from it and will anything else. Thus, when happiness is understood to be the *totum bonum*—the sum of all real goods—it attracts the will with necessity. We cannot will not to seek happiness. Our willing happiness as our ultimate end is not an uncaused act.

All other goods are partial goods. Each one is one good among others. In the presence of such goods as objects of desire, the will is not necessitated, which is another way of saying that its choice of one rather than another partial good is a free choice on its part. Such indeterminacy on the part of the will is utterly different from the causal indeterminacy to be found in quantum mechanics. But in both cases, the causal indeterminacy does not reduce to chance—the complete negation of causality....

The controversy between the determinists and the exponents of freedom of choice goes beyond the denial and affirmation of that freedom. It concerns such questions as whether moral responsibility, praise and blame, the justice of rewards and punishments, depend on man's having freedom of choice.

QUESTIONS ON "FREEDOM OF CHOICE"

1. What is the misunderstanding that Adler sees as the basis of determinism?
2. What argument for freedom discussed in this Chapter is discussed by Adler?

Notes

1.   See Joseph Donceel, S.J. *Philosophical Anthropology* (New York: Sheed and Ward, 1969), 371.

2.   Aristotle, *Nicomachean Ethics* III 1109b30-1110b.9.

3.   See Milton A. Gonsalves, *Fagothey's Right & Reason Ethics in Theory and Practice*. Ninth Edition. (Columbus, OH: Merrill Publishing Co., 1989), 32-38.

4.   Aristotle, *Nicomachean Ethics* I 1094a1.

5.   See Donceel, *op. cit.*, 373ff.

6.   *Ibid.*

7.   Aristotle, *Nicomachean Ethics* III 1112a18-1112b11.

8.   Thomas Aquinas. S.T. I, q. 83, a. 1, resp.

9.   See *The Cambridge Companion to Stoicism* (Cambridge, U.K.   New York: Cambridge University Press).

10.   See Donceel, *op. cit.*, 370.

11.   B.F. Skinner, *Beyond Freedom and Dignity* (New York: Knopf, 1971) passim.

12.   *Ibid.*, 19, 27-28, 42.

13.   Edmund O. Wilson, *On Human Nature* (Cambridge, MA: Harvard University Press, 1978),75-78,

14.   David Suzicki and Peter Knudson, *Genethics* (Cambridge, MA: Harvard University Press, 1990), 123-141.

15.   Suzicki and Knudson, *op. cit.*, 123.

16.   See "Temperament" in *New Catholic Encyclopedia*. (New York: McGraw Hill, 1967).

17.   Duns Scotus: Oxford Commentary. Book II. D. 25 response.   Cited in Hyman and Walsh, *Philosophy in the Middle Ages*, (Indianapolis: Hackett Publishing Company, 1973), 641.

18.   John Paul Sartre, *Being and Nothingness*, 627.

19.   Sartre, *op. cit.*, 440-41, 481, 610-6.

20.   John Paul Sartre, *Existentialism is a Humanism*, in Kreyche, Mann, op. cit., 595-96.

21.   See Francis Lescoe, *Existentialism: with or without God* (New York: Alba House, 1974), 284-85.

22.   C.S. Lewis. *The Four Loves* (New York: Harcourt Brace, 1960).

23.   Reprinted with the permission of Scribner, a Division of Simon & Schuster Adult Publishing Group from *Ten Philosophical Mistakes* by Mortimer J. Adler.   All rights reserved, 147-151.

Chapter 5

HUMAN DUALITY

The title of this Chapter sounds a little strange, but the idea is familiar. We humans are both physical and mental. Aristotle's definition of us as rational animals highlights that fact. Our own language is deeply dualistic. We speak of mind and body or body and soul. We talk about thoughts and ideas, hopes and worries—things that are "on our mind." We talk about our arms and legs, stomachs and eyes and ears, the physical parts of our body. We care about our appearance and are concerned for the health of our bodies. But the care and concern are not bodily events, but part of a private mental life which we can communicate to others by words. We eat, drink, we do physical activities of every sort, walking, playing games, chopping wood, or having sex. We also engage in mental activities like planning our day, reviewing our behavior, deciding what to wear, thinking over a problem. Making up your mind is real, but it is not physical in the way making your bed or making up your face is.

TWO DUALISMS

Much work in philosophy has been done in an attempt to explain the nature and operations of the two parts of the human. Plato was the first to elaborate in any great length a dualism. *Dualism* is defined as: *the view that the human being is composed of two parts, a spiritual part called mind or soul, and a physical part called body*. Plato thought of the dualism of humans as a misfortune, an unnatural state, an obstacle to genuine knowledge. He wrote:

All these considerations, said Socrates, must surely prompt serious philosophers to review the position in some such way as this. It looks as though this were a bypath leading to the right track. So long as we keep to the body and our soul is contaminated with this imperfection, there is no chance of our ever attaining satisfactorily to our object, which we assert to be truth. In the first place, the body provides us with innumerable distractions in the pursuit of our necessary sustenance, and any diseases which attack us hinder our quest for reality. Besides, the body fills us with loves and desires and fears and all sorts of fancies and a great deal of nonsense, with the result that we literally never get an opportunity to think at all about anything. Wars and revolutions and battles are due simply and solely to the body and its desires. All wars are undertaken for the acquisition of wealth, and the reason why we have to acquire wealth is the body, because we are slaves in its service. That is why, on all these accounts, we have so little time for philosophy. Worst of all, if we do obtain any leisure from the body's claims and turn to some line of inquiry, the body intrudes once more into our investigations, interrupting, disturbing, distracting, and preventing us from getting a glimpse of the truth. We are in fact convinced that if we are ever to have pure knowledge of anything, we must get rid of the body and contemplate things by themselves with the soul by itself. It seems, to judge from the argument, that the wisdom which we desire and upon which we profess to have set our hearts will be attainable only when we are dead, and not in our lifetime. If no pure knowledge is possible in the company of the body, then either it is totally impossible to acquire knowledge, or it is only possible after death, because it is only then that the soul will be separate and independent of the body. It seems that so long as we are alive, we shall continue closest to knowledge if we avoid as much as we can all contact and association with the body, except when they are absolutely necessary, and instead of allowing ourselves to become infected with its nature, purify ourselves from it until God himself gives us deliverance. In this way, by keeping ourselves uncontaminated by the follies of the body, we shall probably reach the company of others like ourselves and gain direct knowledge of all that is pure and uncontaminated—that is, presumably, of truth. For one who is not pure himself to attain to the realm of purity would no doubt be a breach of universal justice.[1]

Plato states that the care of the body is an "imperfection," which contaminates the soul. He says the body and its cares are a distraction to the soul, often keeping it from being able to think. Genuine knowledge will come only when we get rid of the body. Getting rid of the body is described by him as "deliverance."

Plato believed that the soul, a purely spiritual substance, pre-existed the body. He believed that the soul dwells in the body as in a prison and is destined to be freed from the body and return to the Heaven from which it came.[2] In fact Plato believes that the imprisonment is willed by God, and Plato uses that consideration as an argument against suicide, which releases the soul from its jail, the body, without God's permission.[3]

Plato's viewpoint of the body-soul relationship can be described as *exaggerated* or *extreme dualism.* Such a dualism is defined: *the view of the human being that sees the human as constituted of a union of two separate and distinct parts, one of which is spiritual and the other, material.* Although body and soul coexist in the living human being, they do not form a natural union, but rather a forced togetherness. Their relationship is the physical closeness of the horse and rider alongside each other, but not of two parts comprising a genuine whole.

We have already seen the limitations of Plato's rationalistic approach to knowledge. In his description of the relationship of soul and body, Plato does sound notes which resonate with human experience. Worrying about our health does interfere with our ability to think about things. Being in love, or working eighty hours a week selling advertising or computers, are emotional and physical factors that inhibit the pursuit of truth. But it is quite a leap to conclude that the body is a "prison" or "contamination" or that we would be better off rid of it.

Aristotle, Plato's pupil who founded his own school because of profound intellectual differences with his teacher, proposed a much closer relationship between soul and body in the human being. Body and soul compose a unitary being. Soul relates to body as its form, that which defines it, enlivens it, actualizes it. He wrote:

> That is why the soul is an actuality of the first kind of a natural body having life potentially in it. The body so described is a body which is organized. The parts of plants in spite of their extreme simplicity are organs; e.g. the leaf serves to shelter the pericarp, the pericarp to shelter the fruit, while the roots of plants are analogous to the mouth of animals, both serving for the absorption of food. If, then, we have to give a general formula applicable to all kinds of soul, we must describe it as an actuality of the first kind of a natural organized body. That is why we can dismiss as unnecessary the question whether the soul and the body are one: it is as though we were to ask whether the wax and its shape are one, or generally the matter of a thing and that of which it is the matter. Unity has many senses (as many as 'is' has), but the proper one is that of actuality.

We have now given a general answer to the question, What is soul? It is substance in the sense which corresponds to the account of a thing. That means that it is what it is to be for a body of the character just assigned. Suppose that a tool, e.g. an axe, were a *natural* body, then being an axe would have been its essence, and so its soul; if this disappeared from it, it would have ceased to be an axe, except in name. As it is, it is an axe; for it is not of a body of that sort that what it is to be, i.e. its account, is a soul, but of a natural body of a particular kind, viz. one having in itself the power of setting itself in movement and arresting itself.[4]

Thomas Aquinas, a thirteenth-century philosopher in his work *On the Soul* agreed with Aristotle's view of the unity of the human and was critical of Plato's extreme dualism. Aquinas wrote:

> But elsewhere Plato maintained that the human soul not only subsisted of itself, but also had the complete nature of a species. For he held that the complete nature of the [human] species is found in the soul, saying that a man is not a composite of soul and body, but a soul joined to a body in such a way that it is related to the body as a pilot is to a ship, or as one clothed to his clothing. However, this position is untenable, because it is obvious that the soul is the reality which gives life to the body. Moreover, vital activity (vivere) is the act of existing (esse) of living things. Consequently, the soul is that which gives the human body its act of existing. Now a form is of this nature. Therefore the human soul is the form of the body. But if the soul were in the body as a pilot is in a ship, it would give neither the body nor its parts their specific nature.[5]

Aquinas agrees with Aristotle on the nature of the soul and on its relationship to the body. The soul is not a physical part, or harmony of bodily parts; it is an intellective, non-material reality able to exist on its own. However, the soul does not when joined to the body exist as a separate unit, as the pilot and the ship. The soul is joined to the body in a unique relationship which is expressed in the formula, "the soul is the form of the body." By "form," Aquinas, following Aristotle, means that which defines the body as a human body. Form is a *forma cause*, namely, *that which makes a being to be what it is.* The *human soul* is: *the ultimate internal spiritual principle which constitutes the human being as a living human.* The soul is not within the body as a separate thing, as a battery is in a doll or toy car, but it is united with the body so as to constitute only one thing, the human being.

Aquinas gives the reason the soul cannot be related to the body as a pilot to a ship, or a battery inside a machine to a machine: that would make the soul the whole human species. It would turn the human into two beings, the human and the body of the human. Aquinas furnishes another reason why the soul cannot be separate from body: the operation of abstraction by which the human mind grasps the intelligible content in a physical object grasped by the senses or held in the imagination.[6] As we have seen in Chapter 3, abstraction involves the bodily senses and the human mind working with one another. If I want to form a concept of square, I must see or feel a square object, at least in imagination.

EVIDENCE FOR MODERATE DUALISM

The dualism defended by Aristotle and Aquinas is called *moderate dualism* and is defined as: *the view that the human being is a composite unity of a spiritual principle or soul and a material principle, the body*. Moderate dualism safeguards the unity of the human being. The evidence for this comes not only from abstraction, as we have seen, but also from language, art and technology, games, and emotion.

Language is: a system of physical signs which express meaning.[7] When humans speak, they take their thoughts and put them in a physical form. The physicality of language is the sounds uttered, words written, figures drawn, or ridges constructed. Language is not a series of noises or marks on paper, but an organized system of symbols. Symbols are physical realities which have a meaning that society has agreed upon. A red octagonal sign with the word "STOP" on it is a conventional sign. The word "Stop" is an agreed upon symbol which expresses the meaning "Come to a halt; cease doing what you are doing." The symbols express something that is interior, invisible, mental—a meaning or idea. For example, the word "know" expresses a certainty about whatever is said to be known. The word "want" indicates the speaker or writer has the desire for something. The word "car" expresses the concept of a motorized vehicle used for transportation.

When we write a word on paper or type it into the computer, it is not just a matter of hand-eye coordination. It is thinking and expressing the thought physically. It is mind and body at work harmoniously. Our phrasing of a question perhaps best exhibits the coordination of mind and body in spoken language, for we formulate what it is that we want to know, and use the words that convey to our listeners that desire for that particular information.

The creation of works of art such as paintings, sculptures, musical compositions, shows our dual character. *Art* is: *the production of something beautiful.*[8] The visual artist, for instance, takes physical matter and changes it by sketching or painting, or carving an image which expresses or evokes beauty or an emotion and an appreciation of the beautiful. The artist aims to please, (sometimes to shock) and his choice of colors and images and shapes is thought out to create that impression. The sketch artist at the county fair, for instance, will talk for a minute to his subject so that the face he limns will evoke something of the personality, the inner self of his subject. Thinking is an inner mental activity. Sculpting a statue with a man resting his chin on his hand is mental and physical. Musical compositions, too, whether sung, played by a single instrument, or by an orchestra, express joy, sadness, enthusiasm, reverence, patriotism, and can stir up those feelings. Every nation has its national anthem; and every church has its hymns. Movies and television build up drama not only by dialogue but by the accompanying music. We couldn't be artists or musicians, or appreciate art or music, unless we were a unity of mind and body.

The human being, as we have seen in our discussion of intelligence, is a producer. We fashion things for our use. We make tables and chairs and beds, hammers, saws and axes, washers and dryers, furnaces and stoves, cars and airplanes, cell phones and computers. We produce things for our entertainment such as toys, television, games, musical instruments. All such productions can be called *Technology* and defined as: *the rearrangement of matter in order to produce something suitable for a human purpose.*[9] In looking at a tree, a human can envision a table, a chair, a bed, or a boat. He can then cut down the tree and shape it according to the vision he had in mind. In making a table, the idea of a flat surface, supported by legs, is embodied in the wood chopped and sawed and glued together. In selecting materials for a house, the builder must understand the strength of the materials and the load they will bear, so that the house stands up and that the second floor supports the family sleeping there.

Furthermore, *using* the objects produced for human benefit reveals how closely mind and body are united. To set a glass down on a table, we have to grasp that the surface is flat and unoccupied, as well as using our arm and hand to deposit the glass. Driving a car is a mental and physical effort, as are everyday activities like setting an alarm clock, getting dressed, putting toast in the toaster, and "channel surfing."

Playing games is something unique to humans. A *game* is: *a competitive activity involving skill or chance, played according to rules, for the amusement of the players or spectators.*[10] Animals exhibit playful behavior, but don't invent sports like baseball and football, or basketball. Animals don't create Scrabble, Monopoly or chess games. When humans play basketball, they don't just bounce a ball on a floor, but share in an activity that involves strategy, interaction with others, avoiding obstacles, and much more. Moving a chess piece is not just transferring a material object from one location to another; it is an action informed by understanding of the context of the game, and the goal of victory. Again, mind and body are working in harmony.

Another significant feature of human life that reveals our duality is emotion. *Emotion* can be defined as: *The affective and bodily response to the understanding of a situation as impacting on one's well being.*[11] Emotion is a feeling state: mad, glad, sad, worried, hopeful, excited, serene, contented, jealous, resentful, bitter. Emotion involves our body, which reacts spontaneously to express the feeling state physically with tears, frowns, smiles, sweat, blushing, tensing of muscles, gritting of teeth, churning of the stomach, quickening of the pulse,, for instance. Emotions are triggered by an understanding of the impact of situations on ourselves. The phone rings. The caller is a friend, we smile, relax. The phone rings, and it is from a stranger trying to sell us something we are not interested in. We tense up, start to feel angry and resentful of the intrusion into our life. If someone is out are out for a walk and sees a snake on the path ahead, he or she will likely react in one of two ways. If she is fascinated by snakes, and sees no threat in them, she will marvel at the color and excitedly move closer. If he is terrified by snakes, the thought of impending danger will cause him to freeze up. If you ace a test, you smile and feel good. If you flunk a test, you frown and feel sad, or mad, or both. All these instances show the human being is one being, not a mind on top of a body, or hidden inside it.

The unity of the mental and the physical in human experience as illustrated by language, art, technology, games, and emotion indicates that humans are not a mixture of substances maintaining their separate identities, but a true composite, as moderate dualists hold.

MATERIALISM

In the history of philosophy there have been thinkers who viewed human beings as being only physical. That view is labeled *Materialism*, defined as: *the view that human beings are only physical beings, and that mental processes like thinking or deciding are only material functions.* The ancient Greek philosophers Democritus and Leucippus and Epicurus were men of this sort. Democritus flourished around 450 B.C. and Leucippus twenty five years later. Their atomistic system—soul and body were both composed of tiny material particles (atoms)—was taken up by Epicurus (c. 300 B.C.) whose teaching has come down to us through the Roman poet Lucretius (c. 60 B.C.). In his poetic treatise *On the Nature of Things*, Lucretius explained and defended materialism. He wrote:

I now declare that mind and soul are joined

together, and form one single entity,

but the head so to speak, that rules in all the body,

is counsel, mind, and intellect, as we say,

and this is placed midway within the breast.

For here leap terror and panic, this spot feels

sweet joy; here, then, are intellect and mind.

The rest of the soul, dispersed through all the body,

obeys the mind and moves to its command.

For mind thinks its own thoughts, knows its own pleasures,

when nothing has stimulated soul or body.

And as when injury attacks our head

or eye, they hurt, but we're not agonized

all over, thus the mind sometimes feels pain

or joy and strength, and when other parts of soul

in limb and joint have felt no novel impulse.

But when the mind is deeply stirred by terror,

all through the body we see the soul affected;

we pale, and over all the body sweat

> pours out, the tongue stumbles, voice goes awry,
>
> eyes are befogged, ears ring, the knees give way,
>
> yes, from sheer terror of mind we often see
>
> men fall in a faint; thus readily we perceive
>
> the union of soul and mind, for soul, when struck
>
> by mind, in turn strikes body and makes it move.
>
> This argument also proves that soul and mind
>
> are physical things. Clearly, they move our limbs,
>
> arouse the body from sleep, change our expression,
>
> and guide and govern the man in all his being.
>
> Yet without touch, we see, such things can't happen,
>
> nor touch without matter; must we not then admit
>
> the soul and mind in act are physical things?
>
> Besides, we see that in our bodies, soul
>
> and body act and react in sympathy.
>
> If a bristling spear has driven deep, exposing
>
> sinew and bone, and yet not taking life,
>
> still faintness follows and sweet swooning down
>
> to earth, and there a sense of rocking motion,
>
> sometimes with vaguely felt desire to rise.
>
> And so the soul must be a physical thing,
>
> since physical weapon and wound can make it suffer.[12]

Lucretius states that the soul is a physical substance dispersed throughout the body, for life exists throughout the body, and soul is associated with life. He speaks of mind as the seat of self-consciousness, decision-making, and the center of feelings. He then equates soul and mind, and argues that they are not a distinct type of substance, but they are material like arms and legs. He offers three arguments. First, the emotion of terror, a mental experience, causes bodily reactions, and since what affects the body is material, the soul must be material. Second, the soul arouses the body from sleep, directs its movement which couldn't be done without the body, so the soul is bodily. His third argument that the mind or soul is material is expressed in the enthymeme, "And so the soul must be a physical thing since physical weapons and wounds can make it suffer."[13] When put into proper syllogistic form, the argument reads this way:

What is affected by physical weapons and wounds is physical.

The soul is affected by physical weapons and wounds.

Therefore, the soul is physical.

A moderate dualist might answer this argument by pointing out that it is not the physical wound or weapon that brings about the worry or concern in the mind. It is rather the understanding of the wound as possibly life-changing or even life-ending. In regard to the influence of terror upon the body, as we noted in our description of emotion, feeling an emotion involves the interpretation of how events might affect us. Interpretation is not a physical event. And the cooperation of mind and body in arousing ourselves from sleep and bodily movement does not imply a unity of one substance, but rather the unity of a composite.

Lucretius continues:

Furthermore, as the body suffers the horrors of disease and the pangs of pain, so we see the mind stabbed with anguish, grief and fear....

Again, when the pervasive power of wine has entered into a man and its glow is dispersed through his veins, his limbs are overcome by heaviness; his legs stagger and stumble; his speech is blurred, his mind besotted. . . Conversely, we see that the mind, like a sick body, can be healed and directed by medicine. This too is a presage that its life is mortal.[14]

In these passages, Lucretius is giving a similar kind of argument as he used in regard to weapons, citing disease, wine, and medicine, material realities which impact on mind, thereby indicating that mind must be physical. In argument form:

If anything material affects the mind in any way, the mind is material.

Disease, wine and medicine, all of which are material things, affect the mind.

Therefore, the mind is material.

A moderate dualist can reply that the arguments of Lucretius are a problem for an exaggerated dualist like Plato who view body and soul not only as distinct, but as separate. For those like moderate dualists who hold that humans are composites of body and soul, interaction is to be expected. For, if understanding, which is non-physical, impacts on the physical sense appetite giving rise to emotions, what is the surprise that disease, wine and medicine have an impact on the soul? Furthermore, one could argue that the effects of disease, wine, medicine are only *indirectly* effects on the mind. They directly impact on the body and brain, but because of the unity of body and soul in the human, the mind is affected by what happens in the body.

The moderate dualist also has his basic argument that the activities of thinking abstractly, reasoning, loving benevolently, desiring peace of mind and justice for all, and being conscious of oneself, are not physical actions, and therefore cannot be explained by something material. Matter is not an adequate cause for an activity that is non-material.

IDEALISM

Materialism is literally a one-sided view of the human being. It is one example of what philosophers call monism. *Monism* is: *the belief that human beings are entirely only one type of reality.* In the eighteenth century, George Berkeley developed a monism that described the human being as purely spiritual. The body is a group of perceptions of a mind. This view is called *idealistic monism* or *idealism* and may be defined: *the view that the human being is made up of only one substance, mind or spirit. Body is a group of perceptions or projec*tions of mind. Berkeley wrote:

> *The existence of external bodies wants proof.*–But though it were possible that solid, figured, moveable substances may exist without the mind, corresponding to the ideas we have of bodies, yet *how is it possible for us to know this?* either we must know it by sense, or by reason. As for our senses, by them we have the knowledge *only of our sensations*, ideas, or those things that are immediately perceived by sense, call them what you will: but they do not inform us that things exist without the mind, or unperceived, like to those which are perceived. This the materialists themselves acknowledge. It remains therefore that if we have any knowledge at all of external things, it must be by *reason*, inferring their existence from what is immediately perceived by sense. But (I do not see) what reason can induce us to believe the existence of bodies without the mind, from what we perceive, since the

very patrons of matter themselves do not pretend, there is *any neces-sary connection betwixt them and our ideas.* I say, it is granted on all hands (and what happens in dreams, frenzies, and the like, puts it be-yond dispute) that *it is possible we might be affected with all the ideas we have now, though no bodies existed without, resembling them.* Hence it is evident the supposition of external bodies is not necessary for the producing our ideas: since it is granted they are produced some-times, and might possibly be produced always, in the same order we see them in at present, without their concurrence. ...

Seventh objection.–Answer.–Seventhly, it will upon this be demanded whether it does not seem *absurd to take away natural causes, and as-cribe every thing to the immediate operation of spirits?* We must no longer say upon these principles that fire heats, or water cools, but that a spirit heats, and so forth. Would not a man be deservedly laughed at, who should talk after this manner? I *answer,* he would so; in such things we ought to *think with the learned, and speak with the vulgar.* They who to demonstration are convinced of the truth of the Coperni-can system, do nevertheless say the sun rises, the sun sets, or comes to the meridian: and if they affected a contrary style in common talk, it would without doubt appear very ridiculous. A little reflection on what is here said will make it manifest, that the common use of language would receive no manner of alteration of disturbance from the admis-sion of our tenets.

In the ordinary affairs of life, any phrases may be retained, so long as they excite in us proper sentiments, or dispositions to act in such a manner as is necessary for our *well-being,* how false so ever they may be, if taken in a strict and *speculative sense.* Nay, this is unavoidable, since propriety being regulated by *custom,* language is suited to the *re-ceived* opinions, which are not always the truest.[15]

Berkeley asserts that there is no such thing as material substance and that humans are spirits. He builds his argument from his analysis of the experience of perception. However, Berkeley sees perception as a per-ception of sensations, not of things. Material objects do not exist except as ideas in minds. Even our awareness of our own bodies is not the awareness of a material object, but is an awareness of the sensation of color, the sensation of warmth, the sensation of length, softness or hard-ness, the sensation of desire, the image of our own knees. Hence, the body is just a group of perceptions in our mind. The human being is a spirit with ideas, not a spirit joined to matter.

Any critique of Berkeley must begin with his theory of perception which is fundamental to his views. Three features of human experience run contrary to Berkley's view of perception: 1. perceptions are shared; 2. perceptions are permanent; 3. perceivers are often acted upon by what they perceive. First, if a student in a class waves her hand to draw the teacher's attention, those seated around her who are looking can see her hand just the same as the teacher can. All students share an awareness of the teacher as male or female, old or young, white or black. If the teacher calls out "John "or "Mary", everyone listening hears the words "John" or "Mary." We could bring in people from Europe, Asia or Africa, and ask them if they could sere the raised hand as the teacher and other students do, hear the sound of "John" or "Mary" as all present do. Although our emotional relationships with self and others, and our subjective bodily states can impact on the way we perceive—some students might see the teacher as taller than he really is—yet we do live in the same world of people, water, earth, sun and moon, trees and houses and cars and cell phones.

Second, our perceptions are permanent. The face I look at in the mirror is the same color every day, eyes and nose are in the same position. The teeth I brush are mine, same as they were yesterday. The legs I put into pants are the same as yesterday's legs. If I cut myself while shaving, it is not just a perception that is different, but a face that is different. If a young woman piles her hair on top of her head, or ties it in back in a pony tail, it is the location of her hair that is changed, not just her own perception of its location. Our bodies are always with us, they are us. They are not just a sum of assorted feels, smells, sights, sounds; rather, our bodies are unified persistent realities.

Third, we are impacted on by what we perceive. Fire warms us, drink relieves our thirst, noises startle us, stings give us pain. Hugs and kisses console us. My hands remove a tear from my face, or put water on it to wash it. In getting dressed, I move my limbs to get my clothes on. In my back exercises, my hands move my knees to my chest. If my hands were perceptions, how could they move my knees? If our body is only a group of perceptions, how is it that different pains exist. When my muscles ache, or I feel a pain in my side, my body is impacting on me, my perceptions are different, because my body is different. When I don't eat and lose weight, or eat a lot and gain weight, am I just seeing different numbers on the scales? If bodies are only some form of mental projection, how does reproduction take place? Is breathing simply a matter of changing perceptions, or is it a change of air?

Since Berkeley's view of the human as just mind depends on his view of perception, the weaknesses of that theory just highlighted remove the foundation for his idealism. In addition, the inability of Berkeley to explain human action like the conscious movement of arms and legs in walking briskly, reveals the weakness of his idealism. A contemporary critic has written:

> Basically what is wrong here is that Berkeley has no way, consistent with his immaterialism, of giving an account of physically doing something which is distinguishable from being involved in a physical happening: doing requires having fingers, arms, legs, muscles, sinews and all the rest in a way that is not reducible to ideas of sense, or possibilities of sensation. Not only do we, in doing, have to think of our bodies as being active in a way in which on the Berkeleian scheme they cannot be; but also, in doing, our bodies have to *be* active in a way in which on the Berkeleian scheme they cannot be.[16]

Neither the idealistic monism of Berkeley nor the materialistic monism of Epicurus/Lucretius does justice to the complexity of human nature. Each is an extreme, reducing all to matter or to mind. Dualism recognizes that humans are both material and spiritual. The exaggerated dualism which we examined in Plato and all exaggerated dualisms cannot explain the close connection of mind and body in the human abilities of abstraction, forming and using language, creating art and technology, playing games, and experiencing emotions. A moderate dualist position on the human is warranted by this evidence.

REVIEW QUESTIONS

1. What are some evidences for dualism based on your own experience?
2. What is the best argument for moderate dualism? Explain.
3. What First Principle does materialism violate? Explain.
4. How are some arguments against idealistic monism "reductions to the absurd"?
5. How might the idea of psychosomatic illness support moderate dualism?
6. What philosophical question is involved in the discussion of whether there is such a thing as "mental illness"?
7. What philosophical question is related to the dispute between some forms of monism and dualism?

THE SOUL AS SUBSTANCE AND FORM[17]
LARRY AZAR

Our doctrine that the human soul is at once spiritual and yet extrinsically dependent upon the body unifies the Platonic and Aristotelian notions of the soul. This position, in fact, is rather unique, for it implies that the human soul is both a complete substance (Plato's view) and the substantial form of the body (Aristotle's hylomorphic teaching). Is such a composite doctrine tenable? Can we achieve what Plato and Aristotle could not? Let us first turn to the Platonic intuition of the soul's substantiality.

From the fact that man by nature is a knower, and from the further fact that the intellect—in knowing by abstraction, reflecting, conceiving, etc.—is acting in a spiritual way, it is possible to deduce that the human soul is in fact a spiritual substance. Since only a spiritual substance can perform spiritual acts, and since the human soul (the intellectual principle) does perform spiritual acts, then it follows that the human soul is a spiritual substance. To state that the soul or its intellect is spiritual is to state that it is not intrinsically dependent on matter; that is, it has a spiritual existence (*esse*). And to maintain that the soul is a form (essence) to which existence is given is to imply that it is a complete substance.

If, as Plato thought, the human soul is a complete substance, what is it doing in a body? To ask this question is to inquire into the validity of the hylomorphic thesis of Aristotle. In other words, we must now explain how the human soul, a complete substance, can simultaneously be the substantial form of the body. Here as elsewhere, in order to ascertain what a thing is, we must observe its highest functions, for a thing acts according to its essence, such that from what a thing *does* we can discern *what* it is. In the case of man, the highest functions are intellectual; and thus man *is* primarily an intellectual substance. Consequently, man's act of existing (*esse*) belongs primarily to his intellectual soul, not to the psychosomatic composite. However, since man has only one act of existing (because he is only one being), and since this existence belongs primarily to his soul, then it needs be that this same existence is communicated to his body through the soul. The body can therefore be said to participate in the existence of the soul.

The human soul, then, is primarily a substance, a subsistent form, a divine image. However, the human soul is of such a nature that it cannot perform its proper work without the help of the body. For example, man cannot even form a concept without depending upon data received from the body: although abstraction is performed by the intellect alone as efficient cause (on account of which the intellect is intrinsically independent of matter), abstraction implies a phantasm (on account of which the intellect is extrinsically dependent on matter). Even in reflecting—when, for example, I know that I know this is a book—I must use my senses: I must *see* or *touch* the book. Hence, without the senses, there would be no reflecting. Further, when, upon looking at any apple, I formulate an idea of it, I must use my eyes to see it (or I must *sense* it in some other way, as by tasting or touching it) *before* I can conceptualize the apple. Without the senses, conceptualizing would be impossible. And to the degree that the senses are impaired (congenital blindness, etc.) intellectual growth is stunted. The intellect requires the senses, and the senses imply a body. Moreover, the senses require metabolism, etc. to maintain the body in proper working condition. Even vegetative functions are required to complete man as a spiritual being. Spirituality is not something superadded to a plant or to an animal to produce a person, but the reverse. Man needs sense powers because he himself is an imperfect intellect. *Man is an intellectual substance that can do his intellectual work only by abstracting from sensible species* (sense perceptions, phantasms). Without phantasms, man would have no intellectual knowledge. Although the human soul is an intellectual substance, it could not perform its intellectual acts—it could not know—without the body. While subsistent, *the soul is nevertheless dependent upon the body in its operations*. The soul does not have sense powers because it is joined to a body; the soul is rather joined to a body because the soul has sense powers which are needed for man's intellectual activity. Consequently, to perform its natural work, the human soul must unite itself to the body in such a way as to constitute, with the body, a *natural union*. The intimacy or continuity of intellect and senses in the act of human knowing means that the union of soul and body itself must be an intimate or continuous one. *The soul must be united to the body to form a substantial union.* The natural affinity between the body and the soul in human knowing implies that the soul cannot be only accidentally united to its body; the union cannot be like the union of a rider with is horse, or of a sailor with his ship. Rather, the union must be an *intrinsic* or *natural* unity. In a word, the soul must be united with its body *as its substantial form*. The human soul is therefore *both a substance and a form*.

It is precisely because it is the *kind* of substance that it is that the human soul is also the substantial form of the body. While it is true that *every* soul (including that of plants, animals, and men) as a substantial form is necessarily joined to matter (as insisted upon in Aristotelianism), it is Aquinas' insight that *the human soul must be united to the body—not merely as a substantial form—but especially as a spiritual substance.* The very *essence* of the human soul *as a spiritual substance* demands that it be the substantial form of the body. Man is not so much an animal endowed with reason as a reason (or intellect) endowed with a body; not so much a "soulified body" as a "bodified (or incarnate) spirit."

QUESTIONS ON "SOUL AS SUBSTANCE AND FORM"

1. Explain how the soul is "form" of the body.
2. How does Aquinas' view of humans differ from that of Plato?
3. Find two quotes that establish Azar's moderate dualism.
4. How does Azar add to the discussion of moderate dualism?

THE MEANING OF MAN[18]
RUDOLF HARVEY

The materialists tell us that man is a robot whose accomplishments are the automatic reaction of his impulses to the stimulus of environment. His achievements are neither culpable nor laudable, since he could not, in any given instance, do otherwise than he has done. No one blames iron for rusting. Materialists say that what we naively call mind is a label for the manner in which our complicated nervous systems respond to what is going on about us. Our vaunted rationality is the end-result of all the conditioning which has affected our own life and the lives of our forebears. Man is what he does, and all that he does is but a response to what has been done to him.

This bleak view of human beings has within it an element of truth. While a friend who knows us intimately can chart with fair accuracy our predictable behavior-pattern, still we realize that at any time we may choose to kick over the traces. And if there is one thing that matter cannot do, it is choose. Matter cannot change its mind, for it has no mind to change.

For the materialist matter is primary and plenary, and apart from it there is nothing. Matter is all there is. Nothing exists anywhere that cannot be explained by physical and chemical laws if only we knew them. Thought is the product of neurological changes in the material brain. Moral responsibility is meaningless apart from the customs, habits and interests of mankind. Since man is the highest form of matter, nothing is higher than man. Since necessity is the law of matter, human freedom is an illusion. All that men call immaterial is the product of their imagination which is itself a function of the material brain.

Materialism sells man very short indeed. It sees the lord of creation as a muscular, neural, glandular ganglion with ridiculous illusions of grandeur. His conscience is a species of megalomania. His ideals are as physical as bricks. The universe in which he lives has no purpose higher than his own desires, and God is a human word having no counterpart in reality...

If the materialist is correct and human beings are not fundamentally different from animals, why should they be treated so differently? If human nature is not respectable why should it be respected? If not honorable, why should it be honored? Are all physicians veterinarians? and all educators animal-trainers? How then does a college campus differ from the zoological gardens? Why are there no librarians among the cattle?

QUESTIONS ON "THE MEANING OF MAN"

1. Outline two of Harvey's arguments against materialism.
2. What does his critique add to that given in the text?
3. Can you think of another argument against materialism?

NOTES

1. Plato, *Phaedo* 66b-67b.
2. Plato, *Phaedrus* 234e ff.; *Meno*, 81.
3. Plato, *Phaedo,* 62.
4. Aristotle. *De Anima.* II.412a27-412b24.
5. Thomas Aquinas, *The Soul.* Trans. J.P. Rowan (St. Louis: B. Herder, 1959), Art. 1.
6. *Ibid.*
7. See Reichmann, *op. cit.* 129ff.
8. Webster, *op. cit.*
9. Reichmann, *op. cit.*, 142-43.
10. Webster, *op. cit.*
11. See Reichmann, *op. cit.* 174-75,
12. Lucretius, *On the Nature of Things*, Book III Lines 94-97; 136ff.
13. *Ibid,* line 175.
14. Ibid. 136ff; 415ff.
15. George Berkeley. *Of the Principles of Human Knowledge*, Par. 18, 51-52.
16. A.D. Woozley, "Berkeley on Action," *Philosophy* Vol. 60 No. 223 (July 1985), 297.
17. Larry Azar, *op. cit.*, 280-82.
18. Rudolf Harvey, *It Stands to Reason* (New York: Joseph F. Wagner, 1960), 228-29.

Chapter 6

HUMAN INDIVIDUALITY: THE PERSON

Every human being is unique. Even identical twins who have the same DNA are distinct from one another. Human beings have distinct bodies and distinct fingerprints. Every human being has a distinct awareness of themselves, a consciousness of themselves as the source of their words, thoughts, and deeds. Each human has a mind of his/her own, and a power of free choice that creates a moral character. Each human has the ability to relate, bond, network with others. Each human has an emotional life. All of these factors, mind, choice, relationships, emotions contribute to the manifestation of each one's uniqueness. The word "I" expresses our individuality, as does its other form "me"—"a name I call myself" as the song in *Sound of Music* has it.

THE DEFINITION OF PERSON

There is a special name given to the human individual: person. The dictionary defines a person as a human being as: "a man, woman, or child."[1] It further says: "Person: a human being, as distinct from an animal or thing."[2] Rudolf Harvey gives this description of the origin of the word.

> The word "person" is derived from the Latin word *persona* which once meant the mask worn by actors and later, the role played by actors wearing their several masks. Human beings are conscious participants in the unfolding drama of reality. Intellect alone can know the script. . . Since the human will is free, they may follow the script, or by altering their own lines and actions, ruin their part in the play.[3]

The philosopher Boethius in the sixth century defined person: "An individual substance of a rational nature."[4] Thomas Aquinas had this to say about the definition:

> Further still, in a more special and perfect way the particular and the individual are found in the rational substances which have dominion over their own actions; and which are not only made to act, like others; but which can act of themselves; for actions belong to singulars. . . . Therefore also the individuals of the rational nature have a special name even among other substances; and this name is *person.*[5]

Aquinas affirms Boethius' definition, singling out the substantiality of persons, their "rational nature" and their dominion over their actions. We will now examine Boethius' definition word-by-word in order to better understand what a person is. We begin with the noun "substance."

Aristotle stated that a substance is "an independently existing reality," something that exists on its own, and doesn't inhere in another being."[6] A tree is a substance, for although it does exist in the ground, it is distinct from the ground and is not a part of it. The color, height, width, and shape of the tree are not substances, for those features do not exist in themselves. Those traits are called "accidents." Again, a rock is a substance, for though it exists on the ground, it exists on its own and not as a part of anything else. A human body is a substance, while the various parts of the body are not substances, unless severed from the body. A tiny baby is a substance, though it cannot survive on its own. The words "independently existing" mean having an existence of its own, not an existence that is without any need of anything.

Substances are "free-standing" even though they may be supported by something. A flag is a substance, though supported by ropes tethering it to a flagpole. A bird is a substance, though it is supported by a limb, or the ground, or by air. A man, woman or child is a substance, although each is supported by the ground they walk on, and the air they breathe.

Substances have constancy. Their features may change—the tree loses its leaves which, prior to falling off, change color. The rock is eroded by weather, or changed by human industry, for instance, by being arranged to form a fence. A human body can grow larger or smaller, mature or deteriorate, or lose parts yet it remains a human body.

A substance is always something definite, an oak tree, a pond of water, a cat or dog. When we describe something as a "whatchamacallit" we are indicating our inability to pinpoint its exact nature or give it a name.

To be on one's own as a substance is to be something: a bird, or plane or Superman.

The word "individual", in its root meaning, signifies "not divided." An individual has an inner unity that makes it one reality, though it may have hundreds of parts, as complex living beings do. An individual substance is not a mixture like oil and water, a union like a horse and a rider. Individuals have the kind of unity possessed by a piece of marble, a tree, a beaver, or any individual human. An individual is distinct from all other beings; it is not a part of anything else. St. Thomas highlights the unity of persons when he offers a creative derivation of the word "*persona*," Latin for person.[7] He says that word is derived from the expression *"per se unum"* which means a unity in and of itself. The Franciscan philosopher Duns Scotus argued that every individual reality had to have a specific feature that made it unique and distinct from every other individual in its species. He called that distinguishing feature "thisness" (in Latin, *haecceitas*). Human beings, in particular, had to have something positive which made them distinct from others, something more than the fact that their bodies were different.[8]

An individual is the source of all its activities. It is the cat who licks up milk, the rock which rolls, the dog who runs, or the human being who thinks of a word, chooses from a menu, feels glad or sad, plays cards, dances, or watches TV. Philosophers use the word "subject" to describe this permanent reality that is the source or ground of a being's activities. Rolling, licking, eating, playing, dancing and watching are not activities that exist on their own—they are the activities of a being who acts, an individual that persists in time.

RATIONAL NATURE EXPLAINED AND EVIDENCED

"Individual" and "substance" can be said of things, plants, and animals, but "rational nature" is said only of human beings. Their possession of this rational nature distinguishes them from other living beings and objects, and is the basis for their being called persons. A "rational nature" means: *a nature capable of abstract thought and reasoning, of free choice, of entering into personal relationships, a nature composed of the spiritual and the material.* We have examined those features in our previous chapters. But here we wish to focus on the manifestations of those traits which show that human activities go beyond anything that animals have or do. Hence humans alone are worthy of the name of person.

Rationality, as we have seen, enables humans to devise languages to interact with other humans, to work and change nature for their benefit, to develop the fine arts. Although each of these involves working with matter, the activity of working with the matter goes beyond the merely material—transcending it, to use a technical term. In language, we "construct" non-physical structures of grammar and syntax, and we put a thought content in physical form. Moreover, a good deal of this thought content is on a different level than the physical. We speak of human rights and duties; we talk about a future that has not arrived, and a past that has gone. We refer to people or events in places far removed from our present location; we speak of faith and God. By contrast, animal communication is about life's needs, food, escape from predators, reproduction. Animal communication is characterized by sounds and gestures that are instinctive, not learned.

When humans transform matter by building houses and dams, by creating tableware and furniture and clothing, by inventing telephones, computers and television , they are envisioning possibilities, adapting to circumstances, understanding the natures of the material objects they deal with—they are transcending the material. They are not acting in a rote manner dictated by instinct, as beavers who build dams, and birds and insects which construct nests. While humans build bigger and more luxurious homes, there are no upscale spider webs or birds' nests. While humans devise multiple uses for their products, there are no beaver dams that provide electricity or artificial lakes for boating.

What is also very special about human rationality is the fact that we are aware of ourselves, self-conscious, literally. When awake we know we are awake and are walking, eating, reading, or whatever. Consciousness is like a group of mirrors surrounding us, or a security camera constantly operating. Whenever we act, we are aware of *what* we are doing—driving a car, using a cell phone, reading a book. We also know that *we* are doing what we are doing. The normal human has a sense of himself or herself as the source of his/her actions, and as the son or daughter, brother or sister of someone, the citizen of a definite country. This sense of self is something which changes through interaction with others and life experiences.

Our consciousness retains memories of the past, for instance, a baseball game *we* saw, a ceremony like a graduation in which *we* were involved. We can also remember information–some sports statistics and the material presented in our various schoolcourses. Remarkably, we can remember and examine our past actions as to their morality or prudence.

We can and do project into the future—thinking of what we are to say in a speech or conversation that we look forward to. We can day-dream about a future wedding, even without a prospective groom or bride at hand. We can visualize ourselves driving in a shiny red sports car, regardless of our financial status.

The abilities to look back and look forward are far beyond what is physical. They are abilities that have no counterparts in animal consciousness which is immersed in the present.

Our rational nature is one that is *free*, able to act or not act, act in one way or another without being controlled by any outside or internal factors, as we have seen in Chapter 4. In our desires for such non-physical things as admiration, respect, love, honor and justice, we show ourselves to be on a higher level than other living things in our experience. In our choices of actions that go against bodily urges, whether managing our anger, channeling our sex drive, or overcoming the impulse to stay in bed, we tame the physical so as to obtain some non-physical good, like moral decency, education, health.

Our desires and actions express the self that we are, and they manifest the fact that we are persons. In particular, the way we choose to respond to our responsibilities and obligations to others and to ourselves forms patterns of behavior, or habits, and the ensemble of habits shapes our moral character. By doing generous things, we become generous persons. By neglecting to do what we should, we become lazy persons. We acquire a "work ethic" by our choices of disciplined responses to duty. What is more, humans do change character. Decent people deteriorate, because of addictions to drugs or alcohol. Thieves repent of their ways, and become law-abiding citizens. Lazy people become hard-working when they find a person or cause they want to work for.

Moral obligation exists only in the human world. Your cat is not responsible for scratching the furniture, but your 12 year-old son is accountable for carving his initials on the dining room table. Female animals have no obligation to stop another animal from impregnating them, but human females quite frequently do. Owls and hawks do not have conversion experiences and stop hunting squirrels and other small game. Hungry animals eat what they want to eat, when they want to eat. The biggest gets the best. Animal behavior is ruled by instinct, not by choice. Humans have choice, and therefore are responsible for their behavior and are subject to obligations to self-regulate it. Humans don't always control themselves, or do the right thing, of course. But that fact evidences the freedom that characterizes personhood.

Our rational nature, as we have seen in Chapter 2, is a *social* one. We are inclined and desire to interact with other humans. We are born into families, and form societies. We invent languages for communication and tools for communication like telephones and computers. We form friendships and voluntary associations of all sorts. Human sociability is special in several ways that we have not yet discussed: 1.its intelligence, 2.its freedom, and 3. its emotionality.

First, human interaction is intelligent, as illustrated by the use of language, invented to communicate with other humans. Humans further invented communications devices like mail, telephones, the telegraph, e-mail, text-messaging to interact with others not physically present. Humans invent games to play with other humans; humans solicit and get the help of others in building houses, roads, bridges, skyscrapers. Humans surround a learned man to learn from him, and assemble groups of the learned to inform them in schools. Humans invent businesses and unions, fraternal organization and teams, dances and dates to be with others. Human interaction is ruled by etiquettes of all sorts—manners, team or club rules, laws—all designed by human intelligence to facilitate human interaction. "First come, first served;" "Stand behind the yellow line;" "Major credit cards accepted;" are just a few samples of how we invent ways to regulate our relationships with one another. We designate special times to interact with others, birthdays, anniversaries, retirements, funerals and weddings. These occasions and the etiquettes connected with them are learned, they are not instinctive, as is the case with animal interactions.

Second, the vast majority of human relationships are freely chosen, and the exercise or non-exercises of those relationships which are not chosen is governed by freedom in adults. We choose new friends, discontinue seeing old ones; we join the Elks or the K of C, the Daughters of the American Revolution, or the League of Women Voters. We join a bar association or medical association, a bowling league, or a ski club. Though we don't choose all those whom we will work with, be in class with, be fellow citizens with, or members of an audience with, we do, within these groups, exercise our preference and interact with some more frequently than others. We don't pick our family, immediate and extended, but we choose to have more or less contact as we grow older. With our friends, we can call them, or not, see them twice a year, or every week, talk every day, or once a month. To bind ourselves to interactions we do form clubs with weekly or monthly meetings, dance or karate classes. We can study by ourselves, but sometimes choose to do it with others and form study groups. It is an intelligent thing to do, and it is possible because we have freedom. The freedom we exhibit in our socializing is something that reveals as truly persons, not mere animals who interact by instinct and physical necessity.

Third, human sociability feeds on emotionality. Obviously true of romantic relationships, it is also true of friendships created and sustained by affection, whether for one another or some common interest or pastime like shopping or baseball. Together, humans enjoy emotional experiences of excitement, elation, wonder, surprise, sadness. They do this by attending plays, concerts, sporting events and religious ceremonies Reading groups and book clubs, bird-watchers and hikers, tours and pilgrimages are ways that humans seek out experiences that will satisfy emotions or evoke them, and they choose these experiences with groups. Furthermore, humor and playful teasing are deliberately chosen techniques that enable people to interact with one another in a positive emotional way. Humans mourn together, expressing their grief and sorrow and compassion, at wakes and funeral services of all sorts, which may involve musical tributes, poetry, eulogies, or just person to person hugs. In all these interactions, humans are going beyond the material, living at a level superior to any other animal, interacting as persons.

Although there is nothing intrinsic to the meaning of "rational nature" that includes duality—a pure spirit or angel is intelligent, free, and social—the only rational nature in our experience is human nature, Since humans do physical material things like eating, sleeping and reproducing they have a material part. Since they do spiritual things like reasoning, deliberating, deciding, desiring what is non-material, they have a spiritual component. That the spiritual and the physical form one unified being we have shown in Chapter 5 by examining language, games, art, technology, and emotion. This close linkage between the spiritual and the physical is further shown by the effect of physical illness on mental performance, and the effects of mental state on our bodies, effects called "psychosomatic illness."[9]

HUME'S CONCEPT OF SELF

As usual in philosophy, there are some who deny that humans are persons, or that there is a persistent self which is the ground of the individual's mental and physical activity. David Hume, an eighteenth century sensist, materialist, and skeptic, wrote this:

> There are some philosophers who imagine that we are every moment intimately conscious of what we call our self; thus we feel its existence and its continuance and we are certain beyond the evidence of a demonstration both of its perfect identity and simplicity... But for my part, when I enter intimately into what I call myself, I always stumble on some particular perception or other of heat or cold, light or shade, love or hatred, pain or pleasure. I never can catch myself at any time without a perception and never can observe anything but the perception.[10]

Hume's claims are obvious. We don't have a direct feeling that is a self-feeling or perception, therefore, the self is not real. His view of self flows from and is in accord with his sensist approach to knowledge that says all meaningful ideas can be traced to a physical sensation. In reply, we can say that I know that I am the source of the thoughts and emotions and actions that I experience. The awareness of the self acting is concomitant with the experience of whatever sensation, feeling, thought or action may be going on. I own my actions and often resent it if someone else meddles in something I am doing, whether cooking a meal, arranging flowers, or trying to fix a car. Hume himself took pride in being the author of his books, and rewrote them in order to achieve more notoriety! Again, humans *know* that actions require an agent—you can't have eating without an eater, singing without a singer (or I-Pod), thinking without a thinker.

Roderick Chisholm, a contemporary philosopher, has argued that Hume's notion of the non-observability of the self is flawed, reinforcing the point just made, when he writes:

> It is not the idea of the perception of love and hate or the perception of cold or warmth, much less an idea of love or of heat and cold. It is the idea of that which loves or hates and of that which feels cold or warm (and of course, of much more besides). That is to say, it is an idea of an x such that x loves and x hates, and such that x feels cold and x feels warm, and so forth.[11]

Another argument that supports the existence of a persistent self is patterned on the ethical argument for freedom. If there is no self, there is no praise or blame, worth or dishonor, right or wrong. Moral evaluations do exist, so there must be a self. A self-contradiction also emerges from

Hume's reasoning. For his view that all meaningful ideas must be traced to sensations is not itself traceable to a sense impression or experience, and so is without significance on Hume's own terms. Also, it seems questionable whether the very concept of sensation or perception can be understood as a pure experience, one that does not involve a subject. And we could not detect changes in sensations as we do, unless the sensing subject continued to exist.

PANTHEISM'S VIEW OF THE SELF

Another view of the self that also effectively eliminates the self is the theory of pantheism, which defines everything as God, and reduces the individual to a manifestation of a greater spirit or an illusion. The former approach is that taken by Hegel and the latter by mystical thinkers of the East.[12]   Both viewpoints seem to suffer from a fundamental defect: they end up destroying the very evidence from which their inquiry started, namely, individual human beings and their experiences, of knowing, choosing, and acting. The pantheistic view of the self is vulnerable to another ethical argument: If God is the source of all actions, then no action is good or bad, no agent is really responsible for what happens, because human behavior unfolds with the necessity of the tides. A position with such absurd consequences cannot be true.

Person, Personality, and Character

Humans are persons, but we have a personality and a character. Personality is defined by Webster: "The visible aspect of one's character as it impresses others"; and "the sum total of the physical, mental, emotional and social characteristics of the individual."[13] The word "visible" in the first definition really means publicly noticeable, not detectable with the eyes. The second definition takes for granted that all the characteristics are somehow patterned into a unity—or in cases of what psychologists call multiple personality, several unities. One acquires a personality by life experiences and one's interaction with life experiences, interaction that is conscious and free, as well as interaction that is unconscious and un-free.

That we are persons means that we are the enduring subjects of all our activities, whether or not they spring from one unified personality or many. That we are persons never changes, while our personality often does change. We grow to maturity and acquire poise and self-confidence we did not previously have. We are tested by life's difficulties, financial, child-rearing, illness, and thereby may develop stamina and courage. Our personality can deteriorate due to addiction to drugs or alcohol, or the influence of people of bad character. To others, we may not seem to be the "same person" they knew; but that is not literally true. Changed folks do not have the same personality they did, but they are still the same persons.

Character is defined as: "the aggregate of features and traits that form the individual nature of the person or thing."[14] In this sense, character is closely allied to personality. Character often refers to the moral qualities of a person. In this sense one can be an upright character or an unsavory character. The first sense of character refers to a "nature" that has developed both as a result of unconscious interaction with experience and conscious choice. The second use of the term refers to a "nature" that is formed by choice. A person is brave or cowardly; truthful or deceitful; faithful or unfaithful. Character, because it is rooted in repeated choices, has permanence about it. However, since we are free, we can and do act "out of character" on occasion. It is human freedom and intelligence that lead to the formation of moral character, and only humans/persons possess such a character

REVIEW QUESTIONS

1. How do human consciousness and animal consciousness differ?
2. How "unique" are people, actually?
3. Do you think people have a "thisness"?
4. How has your personality changed in the last three years?
5. How would you refute Hume's view of the self?
6. Are people with multiple personality responsible for what they do in any way?

MAN THE PERSON[15]
LARRY AZAR

"Every person born into this world represents something new, something that never existed before, something original and unique." This anomaly of nature, this breach from matter, we have endeavored to describe throughout the pages of this book. Of all the names which can be predicated of this extraordinary animal, "person" seems to be the most proper. Yet, paradoxically, even this term is fraught with ambiguities; to some, even animals have personalities, or at least Simpson and Beck so inform us. Such utterances of eminent biologists are forgivable, for the notion of personality is admittedly psychological rather than biological. Psychologist Allport explains:

"Hence the individuality of man extends infinitely beyond the puny individuality of plants and animals, which are primarily or exclusively creatures of tropism or instinct.... Man talks, laughs, feels bored, develops a culture, prays, has a fore-knowledge of death, studies theology, and strives for the improvement of his own personality. The infinitude of resulting patterns is plainly not found in creatures of instinct. For this reason we should exercise great caution when we extrapolate the assumptions, methods, and concepts of natural and biological science to our subject matter."

That numerous scientists (including psychologists) discuss personality without a clear grasp of its meaning is again understandable in that the notion was early dropped from experimental literature: "With the coming of experimental and empirical study of psychology, the person tended to drop out of the picture because attention was focused on analytic data, separate sensations, images, and feelings. This way of approaching psychology was criticized by William James in his famous chapter of "The stream of thought?" [*Principles of Psychology*, Vol. I, pp. 224-255.]"

However, the importance of the notion of the person has been reaffirmed by contemporary Personalist psychologists, such E. S. Brightman, Peter A. Bertocci, and William Stern. Personalists are strong in their insistence that psychology must be centered about the person, for it is the person who is the subject of experience: fear, love, imagination, judgment, memory—as well as their actions upon other functions (as fear affects hunger or perception)—presuppose a being, a person who is the agent of such psychological activity. This emphasis on the person as the subject of behavior marks a strong resemblance between Personalist psychologies and phenomenology.

Why is it that man—that peculiar phenomenon that is closest to us—is understood in so many different ways? It would seem that the diverse interpretations of the meaning of man stem from the very complexity of man himself. Accordingly, an accentuation of one type of behavior will depict human nature differently than will an emphasis on another aspect of human conduct. The richness of being, and especially of human beings, is the basis of diverse and even contradictory opinions on human nature. For, indeed, man is a paradox, a seeming contradiction. On the one hand, man is a meager creature, very frail and weak. (The strength of an elephant or mule is often preferable.) Quantitatively, man is a mere drop in the ocean, an infinitesimal nothing. He is the last thing to have appeared in the massive drama of creation, as testified to by anthropology and paleontology. His existence is precarious. Yet, while of less worth than the things around him, man is, from another point of view, the greatest, the most notable of his surroundings. What organic being except man can become aware of what he is and what everything else is? The best specimen of a tree cannot become a dendrologist; the best fish never becomes an ichthyologist. Man's magnificence is that he can know himself and other things, and in his own life develop a culture or civilization. In the words of Erich Fromm, "Man is gifted with reason; he is *life being aware of itself*; he has awareness of himself, of his fellow man, of his past, and of the possibilities of his future." In similar fashion, biologist John Eccles refers to "the mystery of our being as unique, self-conscious existences." The reason for man's uniqueness is spelled out: "Man is unique because he alone has come to recognize his existence as a self." Eccles, be it noted, does not wrap his message in opaque language; he tells us unambiguously that "the conscious self may be identified as the soul.... This component of our existence ... is non-material, and hence is not subject in death to the disintegration that affects...both the body and the brain."

Man is a paradox in that each man feels himself to be an autonomous individual. Each person is as valuable as any other; each is a unique entity and is essentially independent. Nonetheless, he is simultaneously most dependent upon others. He needs the butcher and the baker, a mother, and a wife. He wants both freedom and security. While a law unto himself, in the very roots of his existence he is social, so much so that to cut himself off from his fellowman would be his denouement: "Hence it is evident that the state is a creation of nature, and that man is by nature a political animal.... But he who is unable to live in society, or has no need because he is sufficient for himself, must be either a beast or a god; he is no part of a state. A social instinct is implanted in all men by nature." Describing man as a "finite, personal spirit" who must be his very nature live in society, the profound philosopher of Personalism, Max Scheler, in a contemporary setting, concludes that "as a rational spiritual being, he is *objectively* and originally oriented toward that community and realm. He is thus spiritually determined no less originally than in his physical aspect."

Plants and animals, left to themselves in their natural environment, go their own way; they have certain fundamental inclinations which are realized for their perfection. There is no internal struggle, no conflict between one nature and another nature. On the other hand, man from the very start is a mass of conflicts. Like all natural things, he has basic inclinations; there are certain things which are good for man. Yet there are evil things which have a fascination for him. Man does not seem to have only one nature as do plants and animals, for this would imply unity and harmony of inclinations which would smoothly work toward his ultimate goal. It is quite natural for man to develop only with difficulty. Obviously, there cannot be in man two natures, for that would imply two beings. Hence the paradox. And there is a further paradox: man finds himself permanent: I am I. Yet, while I remain substantially unchanged, my being is going away from me and also coming to me moment by moment, such that there is never a time when I could assert "I am here and now fully; I am my own completion."

Man's nature impels him outward; the exigencies of his nature coerce him to be *transcendent*: "One must transcend himself, take an outside look at his abilities and desires within a context of meaning that is objective, even cosmic. From this point of view, the capacity for self-transcendence and responsibility becomes the truly significant core of human nature." Man thus projects himself toward other things, and especially to other persons. He reaches out to these through knowledge and love. *To be a person is to know and to love in an intellectual manner.* Such acts *perfect* man. And because knowing and loving are *immanent* acts, a man paradoxically, perfects himself immanently by transcending himself. According to psychologist Erich Fromm, perhaps the most important and most universal motive in human activities "can be called the need for transcendence. This need for transcendence is one of the most basic needs of man, rooted in the fact of his self-awareness, in the fact that he is not satisfied with the role of the creature, that he cannot accept himself as dice thrown out of the cup. He needs to feel as the creator, as one transcending the passive role of being created." So too, Logotherapist Viktor Frankl declares: "Human existence...is always directed to something, or someone, other than itself. I have termed this constitutive characteristic of human existence 'self-transcendence.'" The notion of interpersonal relations means precisely that one person can enter into a spiritual relationship with another person. Two or more persons can thus enter into a *communion* with one another. The one can understand how the other feels about a thing or event; one parent can thus appreciate the joy that another parent experienced on an earlier occasion with her own child. Such empathy or identification means that, in this act of spiritual communion, one person can share another's experience, can view the world from the other's point of view. To do this necessitates becoming the other (non-physically) and seeing the world through the other's eyes. All this is possible because knowledge entails a union wherein the knower *becomes* the known. Accordingly, the more I endeavor to know a person, the more I must become him; and the more I become him, the easier it is for me to establish an empathic relationship. Observe that empathy implies the distinction between the *physical* and the *intentional* (*supra*, Chap. 22): In knowing the other, I intentionally become him. I *am* the other (non-physically). However, since I remain myself physically, empathy implies this distinction whereby I can ignore my physical self and concentrate on my intentional self, on what I am intentionally, viz., the other. Now I experience the world as does the other.

Inasmuch as personality implies a communion with others, to be a person is to be a member of a culture, a civilization. Animals have no civilization because they are not educable: There are schools *of* fish, but no schools *for* fish. Inasmuch as man is the only culture-bearing animal, then education, culture, and civilization are non-reductive. Education implies cultivating the intellect (in the context of knowledge) and the will (in the area of love), thereby rendering a person "cultured." Indeed, human behavior cannot be properly understood without the notion of culture. This was clearly understood by both Hegel and Marx. In our own day, evolutionist Lawrence Dillon acknowledges that "only man possesses a culture that is inherited and added to by each passing generation." As may be surmised, the relationship between personality and culture has blossomed into a complete discipline, psychological anthropology.

This stress on transcendence harmonizes magnificently with that of St. Thomas Aquinas, according to whom a man is in the fullest sense a person when he acts, and especially when he interacts with other persons. Man is most properly a man when he acts through freedom, when he acts morally, when he engenders friendship, when through love he enters into communion with others.

QUESTIONS ON "MAN THE PERSON"

1. What feature do Fromm and Eccles see as central to human person-hood?
2. Explain the idea of human "transcendence."
3. Explain three ways in which humans differ from animals, according to Azar.

NOTES

1. Webster's Universal College Dictionary. New York: Random House, 2001.

2. Ibid.

3. Harvey, *op. cit.*, 228-229.

4. Boethius, *A Treatise Against Eutychus and Nestorius. The Theological Tractatus*. Trans. H.F. Stewart (London, Heimemann, 1918), 85.

5. Thomas Aquinas, *Summa Theologica*, I. q 29. art. 1, Response.

6. Aristotle, *Categories, c.5*, 2a10.

7. Thomas Aquinas, S.T. I, q 29, art. 4, reply.

8. See, *Cambridge Companion to Stoicism* (Cambridge, U.K. New York: Cambridge University Press, 2003).

9. The Journal *Psychosomatic Medic*ine has been published since 1939 and is available on the web. Also see John E. Sarno *The Mind body Prescription* (New York: Hachette Books Group. 2007).

10. David Hume, *A Treatise of Human Nature*. Ed. L.A. Selby-Biggs. (Oxford, Clarendon Press, 1888), 251.

11. Roderick M. Chisholm, "On the Observability of the Self," in *Language, Metaphysics and Death*. Ed. John Donnelly. (New York: Fordham University Press, 1978),138.

12. Hegel, *Phenomenology of Spirit*. See Ed L. Miller, *Questions that Matter* (New York: McGraw-Hill, 2004), 229-233 for a short account of Eastern mysticism.

13. Webster, *op. cit.*

14. Webster, *op. cit.*

15. Azar, *op. cit.*, 310-312.

Chapter 7

HUMAN IMMORTALITY

The first and among the greatest of Western philosophers, Plato considered the question of what happens to the human being after death in great length. Given his view of the soul as a spiritual entity in itself that pre-existed the body, it was only natural that he regarded the soul as surviving the body. A belief in immortality is the backdrop to his theory of knowledge, rationalism, for he asserts again and again that true knowledge can only be fully obtained when we are free from the cares and troubles of the body.[1]

PLATO'S ARGUMENTS FOR IMMORTALITY

Plato assembles several arguments for the immortal character of the soul in the *Phaedo*:

Well, said Socrates, must we not ask ourselves this question? What kind of thing is liable to suffer dispersion, and for what kind of thing have we to fear dispersion? And then we must see whether the soul belongs to that kind or not, and be confident or afraid about our own souls accordingly. . . .

Now is it not the compound and composite which is naturally liable to be dissolved in the same way in which it was compounded? And is not what is uncompounded alone not liable to dissolution, if anything is not?

And what always remains in the same state and unchanging is most likely to be uncompounded, and what is always changing and never the same is most likely to be compounded, I suppose?

Now let us return to what we were speaking of before in the discussion, he said. Does the being, which in our dialectic we define as meaning

absolute existence, remain always in exactly the same state, or does it
change? Do absolute equality, absolute beauty, and every other absolute existence, admit of any change at all? Or does absolute existence in
each case, being essentially uniform, remain the same and unchanging,
and never in any case admit of any sort or kind of change whatsoever?

It must remain the same and unchanging, Socrates, said Cebes.

And what of the many beautiful things, such as men, and horses, and
garments, and the like, and of all which bears the names of the ideas,
whether equal, or beautiful, or anything else? Do they remain the same
or is it exactly the opposite with them? In short, do they never remain
the same at all, either in themselves or in their relations?

These things, said Cebes, never remain the same.

You can touch them, and see them, and perceive them with the senses,
while you can grasp the unchanging only by the reasoning of the intellect. These latter are invisible and not seen. Is it not so?

Let us assume then, he said, if you will, that there are two kinds of existence, the one visible, the other, invisible. . . . and the invisible unchanging, while the visible is always changing.

Are not we men made up of body and soul?

There is nothing else, he replied.

And which of these kinds of existence should we say that the body is
most like, and most akin to?

The visible, he replied; that is quite obvious.

And the soul? Is that visible or invisible?

It is invisible to man, Socrates, he said.

But we mean by visible and invisible, visible and invisible to man; do
we not?

Yes; that is what we mean.

Then what do we say of the soul? Is it visible or not visible?

It is not visible.

Then is it invisible?

Then the soul is more like the invisible than the body; and the body is
like the visible.

That is necessarily so, Socrates.

Have we not also said that, when the soul employs the body in any inquiry, and makes use of sight, or hearing, or any other sense—for inquiry with the body means inquiry with he senses—she is dragged away
by it to the things which never remain the same, and wanders about
blindly, and becomes confused and dizzy, like a drunken man, from
dealing with things that are ever changing?

Certainly.

But when she investigates any question by herself, she goes away to the
pure, and eternal, and immortal, and unchangeable, to which she is
akin, and so she comes to be ever with it, as soon as she is by herself,
and can be so; and then she rests from her wanderings and dwells with
it unchangingly, for she is dealing with what is unchanging. And is not
this state of the soul called wisdom?

Indeed, Socrates, you speak well and truly, he replied.

Which kind of existence do you think from our former and our present
arguments that the soul is more like and more akin to?

I think, Socrates, he replied, that after this inquiry the very dullest man
would agree that the soul is infinitely more like the unchangeable than
the changeable.

And the body?

That is like the changeable.[2]

Plato's first argument is from the soul's simplicity as a spiritual reality. Only things with parts can cease to exist, by the decomposition of
their parts. The soul, as a spiritual reality, has no parts and, therefore,
cannot die, since death is the dissolution of parts that formed a unity.

Plato also argues that the soul is invisible, therefore immortal. Un-
stated, but implied in this line of reasoning, is the fact that what is invisible cannot have parts, and therefore cannot die by the dissolution of
parts.

Plato's third argument likens the soul to what is unchangeable and
intelligible, and then concludes to its immortality. The soul is not observed to grow, or shrink, show signs of aging like gray hair or wrinkles,
so it must not be a physical reality. Likewise, the soul knows abstract
truth and is designed to be aware of what is not material, so it must be
non-material in nature. And if the soul is non-material, it is spiritual,
without parts and immortal.

RICE'S ARGUMENT

Versions of this argument have persisted throughout the centuries. The twentieth century writer, Charles Rice observes:

> Because you are spiritual, it follows that you are by nature immortal—that is, that your soul will never die...To prove that the soul is immortal and will never die we first have to understand what death is. Death is the breaking up of an entity into its component parts. In this sense, graduation brings about the "death" of the unit that was a championship football team. The death of a human being is the breaking up, the separation, of the component parts of that human being. Those component parts are the body and the soul—a material part and a spiritual part that itself has no parts.
>
> The human being dies when the soul leaves the body. After the soul and body have separated, the death of the body occurs; the body decomposes, breaking up into its component parts. The determination as to whether a person has died is essentially a medical and scientific question.
>
> The unifying concept here is that the death of anything is its breaking up into its component parts. But the human soul, being spiritual, has no parts, and therefore, by its nature, it will not die. Father Trese summarized the point well: If the soul is a spirit, it must then be immortal, incapable of death. Because by definition, a spirit is a simple substance, with no parts, no extension in space (Part of my soul is not in my head, and part in my hands, and part in my feet. All of my soul is in every part of me, much as all of God is in every part of the Universe.).
>
> The soul being a simple substance, independent of the limitations of matter, it follows that there is nothing in the soul that can decompose, be destroyed, or cease to be. Death is the breaking up of a living organism into its component parts; but with the human soul, there just isn't anything "to break up." [3]

Rice focuses on the spiritual character of the soul, revealed by its ability to think abstractly, as the ground of its immortality. Since the soul is spiritual, it has no parts and cannot fall apart. He also explains a significant point: that the soul does not depend on matter for its existence, and so doesn't decay when the matter with which it is united decays or decomposes.

THOMAS AQUINAS' PROOF

This latter feature of the soul, its independence from matter, formed the basis of Thomas Aquinas' proof:

> Whether the human soul is incorruptible?
>
> Now if there is a form having an act of existing in itself, then that form must be incorruptible. For a thing having an act of existing does not cease to exist unless its form is separated from it. Hence if the thing having an act of existing is itself a form, it is impossible for its act of existing to be separated from it. Now it is evident that the principle by which a man understands is a form having its act of existing in itself and is not merely that by which something exists. For, as the Philosopher proves in the *De Anima*, intellection is not an act executed by any bodily organ. The main reason why there is no bodily organ capable of receiving the sensible forms of all natural things, is that the recipient must itself be deprived of the nature of the thing received; just as the pupil of the eye does not possess the color that it sees. Now every bodily organ possesses a sensible nature. But the intellect, by which we understand, is capable of apprehending all sensible natures. Therefore its operation, namely, understanding, cannot be carried out by a bodily organ. . . . For example, heat in itself does not produce warmth, but something hot. Consequently it is evident that the intellective principle, by which man understands, has its own mode of existing superior to that of the body and not dependent upon it. . . . Thus, we conclude that the human soul is incorruptible.[4]

Aquinas uses the vocabulary of "act of existing in itself." I think his argument is clearer if we use the language of subsistence. We can put his argument in syllogistic form:

> Subsistent beings are immortal.
> The human soul is subsistent.
> The human soul is immortal.

A subsistent being is one which is free-standing and does not depend on anything else for its existence. A plant is not subsistent, since it needs light and air to live. The human composite is not subsistent, since life must be maintained by food and drink. Any subsistent being is immortal, for it cannot be destroyed or cease to exist because of the absence of what it depends on, and self-destruction would be impossible.

The subsistence of the human soul is proved by its spiritual activities which of their nature are independent of matter. For Aquinas, the primary spiritual activity is knowing in a non-material way, that is, universally and abstractly. We have the idea of a tree, for example, which applies to all things having that meaning, and that idea leaves out particular physical details such as e dimensions and location. The human mind can know any reality, unlike a sensible organ which can only be open to a type of reality as a color, an odor, a sound. Thus the intellect does not depend on matter, and the soul is subsistent.

As we have seen in Chapter 4, the human will is also an immaterial power. Its activity of desiring and choosing what is non-material, like justice, forgiveness, love of another for his/her own sake, is not carried out by any bodily organ, and hence not dependent on the body. Such will acts give further testimony to the subsistent nature of the human soul, and strengthen Aquinas' argument.

There have been in the history of philosophical thought a host of other arguments for immortality, and we will consider several of these. But first we will examine the major objections posed against immortality, objections raised as early as the first century B.C.

ARGUMENTS AGAINST IMMORTALITY

A scathing critique of Plato was written by Lucretius, who, as we have seen in Chapter 5, expressed the materialistic views of Epicurus and his predecessors Democritus and Leucippus. Lucretius wrote:

> Again, we are conscious that mind and body are born together, grow up together and together decay. With the weak and delicate frame of wavering childhood goes a like infirmity of judgment. The robust vigor of ripening years is accompanied by a steadier resolve and a mature strength of mind. Later, when the body is palsied by the potent forces of age and the limbs begin to droop with blunted vigor, the understanding limps, the tongue falters and the mind totters; everything weakens and gives way at the same time. . . .

> Furthermore, as the body suffers the horrors of disease and the pangs of pain, so we see the mind stabbed with anguish, grief and fear. What more natural than that it should likewise have a share in death? . . . Since the mind is thus invaded by the contagion of disease, you must acknowledge that it is destructible. For pain and sickness are the artificers of death. . . .

Conversely, we see that the mind, like a sick body, can be healed and directed by medicine. This too is a presage that its life is mortal. . . . By this susceptibility both to sickness (as I have shown) and to medicine, the mind displays the marks of mortality. . . .

Again, we often see a man pass away little by little, and lose his vital sensibility limb by limb. . . . Since the vital spirit is thus dispersed and does not come out all at once in its entirety, it must be regarded as mortal. . . .

No one on the point of death seems to feel his spirit retiring intact right out of his body. . . . On the contrary, he feels that it is failing. . . . If our mind were indeed immortal, it would not complain of extinction in the hour of death, but would feel rather that it was escaping from confinement and sloughing of its garment like a snake. . . .

Moreover, if the spirit is by nature immortal and can remain sentient when divorced from our body, we must credit it, I presume, with the possession of five senses. In no other way can we picture to ourselves departed spirits wandering through the Infernal Regions. So it is that painters and bygone generations of writers have portrayed spirits in possession of their senses. But eyes or nostrils or hand or tongue or ears cannot be attached to a disembodied spirit. Such a spirit cannot, therefore, be sentient or so much as exist.[5]

The brunt of Lucretius' attack is directed at the view that the soul is a spiritual thing. Implicitly, he grants that if the soul were spiritual, it would be immortal, but he argues that the soul is not spiritual. In addition to his claim that the soul/mind/spirit is material, because it is affected by material objects like weapons, wine, medicines, disease and aging, he also suggests that soul and body share growth and decay together, and therefore both must die together. He argues that if death were the liberating thing that Plato claimed it to be, then people would eagerly die, and not reluctantly surrender to death.

Lucretius does not address head-on the Platonic arguments for immortality that establish the spirituality of the soul from its simplicity, invisible nature, and its kinship to the unchangeable. His approach is to express the theory of the material nature of the soul and to argue that the interaction of body with soul proves that the soul is material just like an arm or a leg and, therefore, mortal.

Lucretius also criticizes what seems to be a key assumption for Plato, namely, the pre-existence of the soul. He points out that if that were the case, we would have some memory of it, though the fact is we do not remember any previous existence. And in the last paragraph of the quotation, Lucretius also criticizes the very idea of the soul's existing after death, suggesting that since the soul could not see, hear, smell or taste anything, it, therefore, could not so much as exist.

Our explanation of Aquinas' argument from subsistence and Rice's recasting of Plato's spirituality argument should make it clear that the doctrine of life after death is not linked essentially to the extreme dualistic view of the human espoused by Plato. We have already pointed out that the influence of material things like weapons, wine, and drugs on the human spirit is indirect, flowing from the fact that the human is a body-soul unit. Furthermore, it is the case that individuals of the same age and body size vary much in their reactions to such physical realities—a professional soldier of 175 pounds reacts differently to a wound than a shopkeeper of the same age and weight. Alcohol and medicine do not always produce the same effects on similar individuals. Also, there is medical evidence that Alzheimer's disease, characterized by damage to the brain, is not always expressed in persons with the disease. An experiment with a group of elderly religious women who remained intellectually and socially active revealed that many had died in their nineties with Alzheimer's Disease in the brain, without any corresponding debilitating effects in their mental capacities or abilities to interact.[6] Likewise, stroke victims and those with brain tumors have recovered abilities that they should not have recovered, given the damage to their brains. Hence, the human spirit cannot be entirely dependent on the body, and material in nature.

In the same vein, the soul and body do not necessarily decay together. Many eighty-year olds are still powerful in mind, yet infirm in body. And, unfortunately, mental maturity does not always keep pace with bodily maturity. Furthermore, the reluctance of people to die is no indication that the soul is not immortal, but rather an indication that we don't like leaving those we love, and are reluctant to enter into experiences that are totally novel to us.

With regard to Lucretius' criticism of pre-existence, a moderate dualist would concur. An immortal soul need not be a soul that always eternally existed, but a soul that once in existence cannot cease to exist. In regard to his argument about the impossibility of existence after death, we can note that at best it proves the impossibility of sensation, but not the impossibility of spiritual activities like thinking and willing which are the primary activities of the soul. Even though abstraction requires something material, the activities of reasoning and deliberating need not. The activities of loving another for his or her own sake, and desiring a spiritual good like peace of mind, or union with God, are not activities requiring a body, so Lucretius' argument that soul cannot exist after death because it would have nothing to do is not valid.[7]

OTHER ARGUMENTS FOR IMMORTALITY

Several other arguments for immortality have appealed to thinkers throughout the ages: 1) the common consent argument, 2) the ethical argument, and 3) the argument from the desire for happiness.

1) Defenders of immortality state the common consent argument this way:

An important and universally held human belief must be true.
The belief in personal immortality is an important and universally held belief.
Therefore, the belief in immortality must be true, and the human does have a life after this life.

That a universally held important human belief must be true follows from the Principles of Intelligibility and Sufficient Reason. If the world is knowable, and everything that is has an adequate explanation, then the human mind must be made to get the truth. And if human minds could be deceived about a universally held and important truth, then there would be something wrong about human nature. We would be among the most ill-equipped beings on the planet, unable to trust our knowing powers.

This objection comes to mind. Humans have been wrong about the flatness of the earth, and the central place of earth in our solar system. Such beliefs, however, did not impact on daily life of most people. For the practical purpose of plowing a field, the earth is flat, and the hours of daylight are the same regardless of what one thinks about the relationship of earth and sun. The fact that humans have been able to correct errors points to the overall trustworthiness of the human mind. That fact also reinforces the argument that in an important matter, deeply significant for human life, the human mind cannot be deceived.

The belief in life after death is important, for it affects the way one lives this life. Belief in a life after death influences one's moral code, it enables one to take reasonable care of health without becoming obsessed with it; it makes the risk of life in exploring new frontiers, or protecting other humans, a reasonable thing.

That the belief in life after death is universal in time and place is evident from history. In Plato's time, the Greeks had a concept of a heaven and a hell where the righteous and the evil respectively dwelt after death. The Egyptians' practice of mummification is testimony to their belief in immortality. The *Tibetan Book of the Dead* offers a way to prepare the soul for transition to the next life. Ancestor worship among the Chinese presupposes the survival of ancestors. Even the belief in Reincarnation common in India supports the idea that this life is not the only life. The belief that proper burial is necessary to prevent the spirits of the dead from wreaking vengeance testifies to a belief in the after-life. The fact that some, like materialists, have denied the existence of personal immortality does not take away the "universality" of the belief, for such disbelief is the exception, like the fact that some humans do not possess much of a sense of humor is an exception to the truism that humans have a sense of humor.

2) The ethical argument for immortality has had two forms over its long history, depending on whether it centers on obligation or fairness. Duns Scotus offers a brief argument for immortality that considers the obligation that humans sometimes have to give up their lives in order to protect and defend others:

> Also in *Nicomachean Ethics* he [Aristotle] says that the brave man must expose himself to death for the state. . . .[8] Now he speaks according to the dictates of natural reason. Consequently the immortality of the soul can be known by natural reason. Proof of the consequence. No one is obliged or even able to seek his complete non-existence for the sake of some virtuous good whether the good be something in himself or in another, or a good of the community, for according to Augustine a person cannot desire non-existence. For, if the soul were not immortal, a person who is dying would be accepting complete non-existence.[9]

What Scotus is arguing is this: If this life is the only life there is, one cannot be obliged to give it up, for such an action would run contrary to the human desire to preserve one's life which makes it impossible to desire non-existence. So strong is the desire to exist that even someone who wants to die because of pain would automatically shield himself from an unexpected blow.

Therefore, since humans do have obligations to risk their lives, even die for others, as soldiers, medical people in a plague, parents for their children, then there must be a life after death to adequately sanction that obligation.

Another form of the ethical argument goes like this:

Life is not fair. Good people often suffer illness and misfortunes of every kind, and evil people live comfortably to a ripe old age. Mass murderers often die unpunished and thieves often get away without being caught. Doctors and nurses caring for plague-ridden patients often die along with their patients. There is a sense of justice in us that thinks: Such things should not be. Evil needs to be punished adequately, and good, rewarded.

However, good and evil are not meted out fairly in this life. Therefore, there must be another life after this in which good and evil receive their appropriate reward or punishment.

This argument rests on the presupposition that there is a moral order to the universe as well as a physical order—an order demanding that we do good and avoid evil, an order requiring that good be rewarded and evil punished. Part of the answer to the perennial question, "Why do bad things happen to good people?" is the doctrine of another life, which allows for things to be corrected and evened out.

3) A third argument that has a long history is the argument from the desire for happiness. Saint Augustine developed it first and other medieval philosophers followed suit. Nearer our own times, C.S. Lewis, a mid-twentieth century writer, offered this version of the argument from the desire for happiness. He wrote:

> There have been times when I think we do not desire heaven but more often I find myself wondering whether, in our heart of hearts, we have ever desired anything else. You may have noticed that the books you really love are bound together by a secret thread. You know very well what is the common quality that makes you love them, though you cannot put it into words; but most of your friends do not see it at all, and often wonder why, liking this, you should also like that. Again, you have stood before some landscape, which seems to embody what you have been looking for all your life; and then turned to the friend at your side who appears to be seeing what you saw—but at the first words a gulf yawns between you and you realize that this landscape means something totally different to him, that he is pursuing an alien vision and cares nothing for the ineffable suggestion by which you are transported. Even in your hobbies, has there not always been some secret attraction which the others are curiously ignorant of—something, not to be identified with, but always on the verge of breaking through, the

smell of cut wood in the workshop or the clap-clap of water against the boat's side? Are not all lifelong friendships born at the moment when at last you meet another human being who has some inkling (but faint and uncertain even in the best) of that something which you were born desiring, and which, beneath the flux of other desires and in all the momentary silences between the louder passions, night and day, year by year, from childhood to old age, you are looking for, watching for, listening for? You have never *had* it. All the things that have ever deeply possessed your soul have been but hints of it—tantalizing glimpses, promises never quite fulfilled, echoes that died away just as they caught your ear. But if it should really become manifest—if there ever came an echo that did not die away but swelled into the sound itself—you would know it. Beyond all possibility of doubt you would say "Here at last is the thing I was made for." We cannot tell each other about it. It is the secret signature of each soul, the incommunicable and unappeasable want, the thing we desired before we met our wives or made our friends or chose our work, and which we shall still desire on our deathbeds, when the mind no longer knows wife or friend or work. While we are, this is. If we lost this, we lose all. . . .[10]

The experience is one of intense longing. It is distinguished from other longings by two things. In the first place, though the sense of want is acute and even painful, yet the mere wanting is felt to be somehow a delight.... In the second place there is a peculiar mystery about the object of this Desire. Inexperienced people (and inattention leaves some inexperienced all their lives) suppose, when they feel it, that they know what they are desiring. Thus if it comes to a child while he is looking at a far-off hillside, he at once thinks 'if only I were there'; if it comes when he is remembering some event in the past, he thinks 'if only I could go back to those days.' If it comes (a little later) while he is reading a 'romantic' tale or poem of 'perilous seas and faerie lands forlorn', he thinks he is wishing that such places really existed and that he could reach them. If it comes (later still) in a context with erotic suggestions he believes he is desiring the perfect beloved. . . .

Every one of these supposed *objects* for the Desire is inadequate to it. An easy experiment will show that by going to the far hillside you will get either nothing, or else a recurrence of the same desire which sent you thither. A rather more difficult, but still possible, study of your own memories will prove that by returning to the past you could not find, as a possession, that ecstasy which some sudden reminder of the past now moves you to desire. Those remembered moments were either quite commonplace at the time (and owe all their enchantment to memory) or else were themselves moments of desiring. . . . As for the sexual answer, that, I suppose to be the most obviously false. . . . On whatever plane you take it, it is not what we were looking for.

It appeared to me, therefore, that if a man diligently followed this desire, pursuing the false objects until their falsity appeared and then resolutely abandoning them, he must come out at last into the clear knowledge that the human soul was made to enjoy some object that is never fully given—nay, cannot even be imagined as given—in our present mode of subjective and spatio-temporal experience. This Desire was, in the soul, as the Siege Perilous in Arthur's castle—the chair in which only one could sit. And if nature makes nothing in vain, the One who can sit in this chair must exist. I knew only too well how easily the longing accepts false objects and through what dark ways the pursuit of them leads us; but I also saw that the Desire itself contains the corrective of all these errors. The only fatal error was to pretend that you had passed from desire to fruition, when, in reality, you had found either nothing, or desire itself, or the satisfaction of some different desire.[11]

Lewis' argument is that a desire flowing from human nature itself cannot be in vain. Humans desire to see, they can see. They desire to eat, they can eat. They desire to know, they can know. But humans have a desire for total and complete happiness. We are always looking for what satisfies us. Even behavior that is self-destructive is a way of looking for contentment. Since this desire is rooted in human nature, unlike learned desires, such as to own airplanes or marry movie stars, be president of the country, it must be fulfilled. However, humans are never completely happy in this life, for there is always something "more" to desire. Hence, there must be another life in which we can obtain the happiness we desire.

EXPERIENTIAL ARGUMENTS FOR IMMORTALITY

In the past two centuries, humans have become fascinated with some non-rational arguments for immortality, arguments based on people's experiences with the dead, or their own experiences of another life.

Historically, humans have believed that the spirits of those who have died live on after bodily death, and over the centuries and around the world people have claimed to have heard from the departed. Often a message comes in a dream.[12] One man recalled his deceased father telling him in a dream where an important document was hidden behind a book on a bookshelf in the family homestead. Sometimes spirits take visible form, as in the case of the appearance of C.S. Lewis to J.B. Phillips.[13] Various methods have been devised to contact the dead from the time of the Greeks who used mirrors, to the Seances of the nineteenth and twentieth centuries. Even today, people claim to have heard voices from their departed ones and websites abound with instructions on how to contact departed ones.[14] While much of this anecdotal evidence may well originate in an overactive and loving imagination, the universality of such experiences suggests there must be some objectivity to them. It is just too neat an explanation to say that we love to imagine the dead as still alive, and our unconscious desires cause us to construct experiences of ourselves being in contact with them.

In the mid-nineteen-seventies, Dr. Raymond Moody wrote a best seller *Life After Life*.[15] In this book, he collected stories of people's near-death experiences. In those experiences, which do happen all over the world, humans are pronounced dead, then find themselves out of their bodies, often going through a tunnel. They see departed loved ones, learn information they did not know, and eventually return to life again, changed people. Some have tried to explain these out-of-the-body experiences as a product of oxygen deprivation or some other natural cause. Seemingly, new information would be not new at all, but drawn deeply from the unconscious. Again, although this may be true in some cases, it would seem unlikely that such an explanation was always true.

More significant an objection is the fact that the person's experiences cannot be shown to be of the *next* life. After all, they "came-back" and were not irreversibly dead, though they appeared dead. Perhaps rather than supporting immortality, such experiences support a dualistic view of the human, that there really is a spiritual part of us that is distinct from, and, at times, separable from our material body.

REVIEW QUESTIONS

1. What do you think is the best argument for immortality, and why do you think it is the best?
2. What is the most crucial objection to immortality in your opinion? Why?
3. Can you come up with a counter argument to the common-consent argument, using the same form of argumentation?
4. Is heroism possible without a belief in immortality?
5. What do you think of the "fairness" ethical argument?
6. Do you know anyone who has seen a ghost or had a near-death experience? Has it changed their life at all?
7. Does the doctrine of immortality require a belief in God? Can you establish immortality without proving God exists?

"TEN REASONS FOR BELIEVING IN IMMORTALITY"[16]
JOHN HAYNES HOLMES

(3) This universal diffusion of the idea of immortality takes on an added significance when I come to my third reason for believing in immortality. I refer to the fact so memorably stated by Cicero. "There is in the minds of men," he says, "I know not how, a certain presage, as it were, of a future existence; and this takes deepest root in the greatest geniuses and the most exalted souls." The leaders of the race, in other words, have always believed in immortality. They are not separated in this case, as in so many cases, from the masses of ignorant and superstitious men by doctrines of dissent. On the contrary, in this case the ideas of the highest are at one with the hopes of the humblest among mankind.

In referring thus to the great names that are attached to the idea of immortality, I would not have you believe that I am making any blind appeal to the concept of authority. I have never seen any reason for arbitrarily separating our minds from the companionship of other minds. There is such a thing, even for the independent thinker, as a consensus of best opinion which can not be defied without the weightiest of reasons. And in this matter of immortality there is a consensus of best opinion which constitutes, to my mind, one of the most remarkable phenomena in the whole history of human thinking. I have no time this morning to list the names of those who have believed in the immortality of the soul. If I did so, I should have to include the names of scientists from Aristotle to Darwin and Eddington, of philosophers from Plato to Kant and Bergson, of poets from Sophocles to Goethe and Robert Browning, of ethical teachers and public leaders from Socrates to Tolstoi and Mahatma Gandhi. There are dissenters from the doctrine, like Epictetus yesterday and Bernard Shaw today, but the consensus of opinion the other way is remarkable. Even the famous heretics stand in awe before this conception of eternity. Thus, Voltaire declared that "reason agrees with revelation...that the soul is immortal." Thomas Paine affirmed that he did not "trouble (himself) about the manner of future existence," so sure he was that "the Power which gave existence is able to continue it in any form." Even Robert G. Ingersoll confessed, as he stood by his brother's grave, that love could "hear the rustle of an angel's wing." In the light of such testimony as this, are we not justified in believing that there is reason for believing in immortality? If not, then we know, with James Martineau, "who are those who are mistaken. Not the mean and groveling souls who never reached to so great a thought. ...No, the deceived are the great and holy, whom all men revere; the men who have lived for something better than their happiness and spent themselves on the altar of human good. Whom are we to reverence, and what can we believe, if the inspirations of the highest nature re but cunningly-devised fables?"

(4) This conviction of immortality as rooted in the minds of men, and the greatest men, brings us immediately to the consideration of human nature itself as evidence for its own survival. Thus, my fourth reason this morning for believing in immortality is found in what I would call man's over-endowment as a creature of this earth, his surplus equipment for the adventure of his present life. If we want to know what is needed for successful existence upon this planet, we have only to look at any animal. His equipment of physical attributes and powers seems perfectly adapted to the necessities of his natural environment. The outfit of man, on the contrary, seems to constitute something like "a vast over-provision" for his necessities. If this life is all, in other words, what need has man for all these mental faculties, moral aspirations, spiritual ideals, which make him to be distinctly a man as contrasted with the animal? If existence upon the earth is his only destiny, why should man not prefer the swiftness of the deer, the strength of the lion, the vision of the eagle, to any endowment of mind and heart, as more adequate provision for the purely physical task of physical survival in a physical world? What we have here is a fundamental discrepancy between the endowment of man and the life he has to live; and this constitutes, if this life be all, an unparalleled violation of the creative economy of the universe. In every other form of life, an organism is equipped to meet the exactions of its immediate environment. Man is equipped for this environment, and also for something more. Why is this not proof that he is destined for something more? As we estimate the length of the voyage of a ship by the character of its equipment, never confusing a little coasting vessel with a transatlantic liner or an arctic exploration steamer, why should we not estimate the length of man's voyage upon the seas of life in exactly the same way? What man bears within himself is evidence that he is destined for some farther port than any upon these shores. What he is in mind and heart and spirit, in the range of his interests and the lift of his soul, can only be explained on the supposition that he is preparing for another and a vaster life. I believe that man is immortal because already the signs of immortality are upon him.

(5) This consideration is basic, and sums up our whole case for immortality as rooted in human nature. But it opens out into other considerations which may well be taken as other reasons for believing in immortality. Thus, I would specify as my fifth reason for believing in

immortality the lack of coordination, or proportion, between a man's body and a man's mind. If these two are to be regarded as aspects of a single organism, adapted only to the conditions of this present life, why do they so early begin to pull apart, and the weakness of the one to retard and at last to defeat the other? For a while, to be sure, there seems to be a real coordination between soul and body, between the personality, on the one hand, and the physical frame which it inhabits, on the other. Thus the child is in nothing so delightful as in the fact that it is a perfect animal. Then, as maturity approaches, two exactly opposite processes begin to take place within the life of the human being. On the one hand, the body begins to lose its resiliency and harden, to stop its growth and become static, then to decay and at last to dissolve. There is a definite cycle, in other words, in the physical life of the individual. There is a beginning, then a pause, and then an end. It is from first to last a process of completion. But there is no completion in the life of the soul. "Who dares speak the word "completed," says Professor Munsterberg, the great psychologist. "Do not our purposes grow? Does not every newly-created value give us the desire for further achievement? Is our life ever so completely done that no desire has still a meaning? The personality of man is an enduring thing. As the body weakens through the years, so the soul only grows the stronger and more wonderful. As the body approaches irrevocably to its end, so the soul only mounts to what seems to be a new beginning. . . .

(7) But this question of the irrationality of a world which would allow death to exercise mastery over a radiant spirit, has application not merely to the individual but also to the race. This brings me to my seventh reason for believing in immortality—a reason drawn from the logic of evolution. There is nothing more familiar, of course, than the fact that this world is the result of a natural process of development which has been going on for unnumbered millions of years. If this process is rational, as man's processes are rational, it must have been working all these eons of time to the achievement of some permanent and worthy end. What is this end? It is not the physical world itself, for the day must come when this earth will be swallowed up by the sun, and all the universe he merged again into the original fire-mist from which it sprang. It is not the works of man, for these perish even as man lives, and must vanish utterly in the last cataclysm of ruin. It is not man himself, for man, like the earth on which he lives, must finally disappear. Is there nothing that will remain as the evidence and vindication of this comic

process? Or must we believe that, from the beginning, it has been like a child's tower of blocks built up only to be thrown down?

(9) We are coming now to ultimate things—to those first and last questions of origins and meanings. This brings me to my ninth reason for believing in immortality—the fact, namely, that all the values of life exist in man, and in man alone. For the world as we know it and love it is not the world as we receive it, but the world as we make it by the creative genius of the inward spirit. Consider this earthly scene with man eliminated! The sun would be here, and the stars. Mountains would still life themselves to the skies, and oceans spread afar to vast horizons. Birds would sing, and leaves rustle, and sunsets glow. But what would it all mean without man to see and hear, to interpret? What do the stars mean to the eagle, or the sea to the porpoise, or the mountain to the goat? It is man's ear which has heard the cuckoo as a "wandering voice," his eye which has seen "the floor of heaven thick inlaid with patines of bright gold," his mind which has found "sermons in stone, books in the running brooks, and good in everything." All that is precious in the world—all its beauty, its wonder, its meaning—exists in man, and by man, and for man. The world is what man has done with it in the far reaches of his soul. And we are asked to believe that the being who sees and glorifies shall perish, while the world which he has seen and glorified endures! Such a conclusion is irrational. The being who created the world must himself be greater than the world. The soul which conceives Truth, Goodness and Beauty, must itself be as eternal as the Truth, Goodness, and Beauty which it conceives. Nothing has any value without man. Man, therefore, is the supreme value. Which is the essence of the Platonic philosophy of eternal life for man!

> "Tell me, then," says Socrates in the "Phaedo," "what is that the inherence of which renders they body alive?
>
> "The soul, Cebes replied...
>
> "Then whatever the soul possesses, to that she comes bearing life?
>
> "Yes, certainly.
>
> "And is there any opposite to life?
>
> "There is...Death.
>
> "And will the soul...ever receive the opposite of what she brings?
>
> "Impossible, replied Cebes.
>
> "Then, said Socrates, the soul is immortal!"

QUESTIONS ON
"TEN REASONS FOR BELIEVING IN IMMORTALITY"

1. Which arguments in the article are also mentioned in this Chapter? Does this presentation enhance the strength of those arguments?
2. Explain three other arguments for immortality given in the article.
3. Which argument do you think is the best? Which is the weakest? Explain.

NOTES

1. Plato, *Phaedo*, passim. See Chapter 3 above.

2. Plato, *Phaedo*, 78b ff.

3. Charles Rice, *Fifty Questions on the Natural Law* (San Francisco: Ignatius Press, 1993), 124-25.

4. Thomas Aquinas, *The Soul*, Art. XIV.

5. Lucretius, *On the Nature of Things*, Book III 175; 476-77; 607, 624, 670.

6. See David Snowdon, *Aging with Grace* (New York: Bantam, 2001).

7. John Duns Scotus argued that the cooperation of the intellect and senses in knowledge in this life was such that one could not affirm that the intellect could function after death without the body. Hence he characterized the any proof for immortality as only probable, not demonstrative, not giving certainty beyond the shadow of a doubt. See Scotus, *Op. Ox.* in Duns Scotus *Philosophical Writings* (Indianapolis: Hackett Publishing Co.), 123ff.

8. Aristotle. *Nicomachean Ethics* III, c. 8, 1117b 8.

9. Duns Scotus, *Philosophical Writings*, 146.

10. C.S. Lewis, *The Problem of Pain* (New York: Macmillan, 1948), 131-133.

11. C.S. Lewis *The Pilgrim's Regress* (London: Geoffrey Bles, 1935), 7-10.

12. See *Psychic Phenomena* (New York: Hawthorn Books, 1958).

13. See Ed. L. Miller, *God and Reason* (New York: Macmillan, 1972), 170.

14. See George N. Merle *Science and Psychic Phenomena.* (New York: Harper, 1978).

15. Raymond Moody. *Life After Life; Investigation of a Phenomenon of Survival of Bodily Death* (Boston: G.K. Hall, 1975). The topic became hot. Two similar works were published shortly: Martin Ebon, *The Evidence for Life after Death* (New York: New American Library, 1977) and Maurice Rawlings, M.D. *Beyond Death's Door.* New York: Thomas Nelson, Inc., 1978). Moody with Paul Perry has written *the Light Beyond.* (New York: Bantam Books, 1988) and *Reunion: Visionary Encounters with Loved Ones*. (New York: Villard, 1882).

16. Excerpted from John Haynes Holmes. "Ten Reasons for Believing in Immortality." *Community Pulpit*, 1929-1930.

Chapter 8

TAKING SIDES

Looking back over what we have considered, the real debate about the nature of humans is whether we are a composite of the spiritual and material, or merely material beings, differing only in degree from other animals on our planet. The *moderate dualist* vs. *materialist* opposition has shown itself in each of the six areas we have discussed: sociability, intelligence, freedom, duality, individuality, immortality. In this Chapter, we would like to treat these topics again. Our emphasis will be on human life and the experiences humans have, without any quotations from philosophers or commentators.

SOCIABILITY

In looking at human sociability, we highlighted the polar opposition between Aristotle and his tradition and the English philosopher Thomas Hobbes who attacked the view that humans were naturally political, that is, social animals. Hobbes was a materialist, but materialism does not necessitate his position on sociability the way materialism implies sensism and determinism. Materialists of our times tend to grant that humans are social, but explain it as just an instance of our animal nature. Desmond Morris, for instance, likens human behavior in offices and organizations to that of chickens in a barnyard.[1] Whence, the expression "pecking order" has become part of our vocabulary. In Chapters 2 and 6, we argued that the variety and complexity of human socializing, its use of language, the freedom involved n it, and its emotional character distinguish human sociability from the instinctive, inflexible, rote behaviors and non-linguistic communications of animals.

Five features of human sociability further distinguish the ways humans interact in contrast to animals: 1. Humans plan their socialization;

2. Humans help one another; 3. Humans educate their young and one another; 4. Humans communicate through mass media; and 5. Humans love to be entertained in groups.

1. Although much social interaction is a matter of circumstance, we devise ways of meeting with others. We have dinners and luncheons, breakfast get-togethers, "Happy Hours," cocktail parties, and for some get-togethers, we have a system of invitations and replies. As we have noted earlier, we celebrate birthdays, anniversaries and holidays with others. Weddings and funerals are social events. In the area of romance, we introduce couples who we think will make a good match to one another. We have dating services to enable us to meet other people .We use the internet to find a date or mate. Sometimes parents arrange marriages for their children. Animals mate circumstantially, whether in nature, or in circumstances contrived by humans. Animals just don't throw parties and mingle for the sake of getting to know each other and for the enjoyment of mingling.

2. Humans help one another, singly and in groups. On a one-to-one basis, a neighbor plows another neighbor out of a snowstorm, gives a colleague a ride to the airport, helps an elderly person cross the street or get into a car. Humans have organized systems of helping—the medical system, the vast number of charitable organizations like Red Cross, American Cancer Society (and all other types of foundations for specific diseases like Lupus or M.S.), the various religious communities devoted to nursing, caring for the elderly and educating the young. Many human societies have developed social welfare systems of helping the needy, whether children, the disabled, the impoverished. When natural disasters like floods, earthquakes and hurricanes strike, humans from all over the world offer assistance to one another. Humans care for other humans, not just their blood relatives. They take up collections and do fund-raisers to help pay medical expenses of neighbors or co-workers. Animals help one another with the instinctive tasks of building nests or hives, or dams, but they don't have Habitat for Humanity or organize benefit concerts for famine relief in Africa.

3. Animals suckle their young, humans educate them. We have pre-school, nursery school, elementary school, high school, college and graduate school. Human parents teach children values and traditions, as well as games that entertain and teach them to get along with others. Human parents delegate most of the education of their children to others, though increasing numbers are choosing this task for themselves in homeschools. Even homeschools do not manage without curricula supplied by organizations, and the home schools conform to norms for learn-

ing set by the states. Humans teach their children things that are not "useful" in any sensible, physical way, such as the history and literature of their country and of the world, how to play a musical instrument, or how to play checkers and chess. The parent-child relationship among humans and the grandparent-grandchild relationship are clearly ones of difference in kind from anything found in the animal world, and not something that is purely instinctive.

4. While herds of animals communicate with one another, as do pods of whales, only humans have devised town criers, newspapers, magazines radio, and television to inform one another about events of interest to them as individuals, or members of particular communities, a city, or a nation. Lawyers, physicians, stamp collectors, and other interest groups have their publications. Humans want to know about other people—their customs, their marriages, their tragedies and problems. Supermarket tabloids and talk shows alike reveal our interest in other people—especially those who are "celebrities." Animals reveal no such interest in one another, so it is clear that our level of sociability is different in kind from the instinctive interactions of animals.

5. We humans like to be entertained together: World Cup Soccer, Super Bowl, the Olympic Games, Wimbledon, the Masters are competitive human events in which millions of humans become involved, thousands as immediate spectators, the rest as participants through radio and television. Humans have musical concerts of every type, which draw thousands. We love parades. We go to the movies with friends, and watch games in sports bars. We text message, and share digital photos. Although technology can now allow us to get entertainment when being by ourselves, our inclination is to share the entertainment experience with another, and on special occasions with many.

Yes, the evidence for a distinctive human sociability is overwhelming. Clearly, our interactions with one another reveal a different kind of social nature than anything found in the animal kingdom.

INTELLIGENCE

Moderate dualists call themselves *moderate realists* when discussing the issue of knowledge and intelligence. Moderate realists see human intelligence as non-material and differing in kind from the knowledge provided by the senses. Materialists hold that all human knowledge is ultimately some form of sense knowledge, that no non-material knowing exists, and that human intelligence is only more of the same ability that is displayed by animals. Materialism in regard to the question of knowledge is called *sensism*.

We have already seen how language, art, technology and humor are features of human life that clearly show that humans have an ability beyond the senses, an ability to think abstractly and understand relationships, to envision what could be. The communication, building and playful activities of animals bear the stamp of instinct and lack the complexity, flexibility, variety, and creative aspects of what humans do. Furthermore, nothing like art (in its widest sense, including music, drama, poetry, literature), is found in the animal kingdom.

At least six other features of human life and action come to mind that show that humans exist with a thought capacity really different in kind from that of animals: 1. conscience and ethics; 2.science; 3.history; 4.religion; 5.professionalism; and 6.culture.[2]

1. Humans know that their actions can impact others. They know what it is to hurt others, and to help them, and they know they ought to avoid the former type of action and do the latter. General rules involving respect for life, truth, family, and property are present in every civilized society, and humans are taught these from their youth. Besides general moral rules, many professions have specific codes of ethics for their field, medicine or law, education. We have safety rules to be followed in manufacturing, transportation, travel. The creation of ethical codes and laws involves an intelligence that far exceeds any sense ability.

Conscience involves knowing moral rules and applying them to one's own situation.[3] Conscience is a judgment that we should do, or omit, or may do or not do a particular action. Conscience may also look back on an action and condemn it, or approve it. Although conscience may be accompanied by emotion, it is not instinctive, but learned. It involves grasping the relationship between our actions and their consequences, or possible consequences, as well as a self-consciousness that points to a unique kind of intelligence.

2. Grounded in the desire to know, humans collect and organize the information about the world that they have learned. We seek to know the nature of the earth on which we live, the elements which nourish us, the various forms of plant and animal life, our own human nature and inclinations. We have geography and geology, astronomy, botany and zoology, chemistry and physics, biology, psychology, and sociology. In most of these endeavors, our goal is just understanding for its own sake—we want to know about the world we live in and ourselves. We can and do know our world, formulating systematic bodies of knowledge about it,

dividing up areas of study so as to master them more easily. Such accomplishments are not sensations or combinations of sensations, but a whole different genre. Humans are scientists, animals are not.

3. Humans have a sense of history. We record what has happened in our world, whether at the local, national, or international level. We build large libraries to store information. We also seek to understand history, to find patterns in it, as St. Augustine, Karl Marx, and Arnold Toynbee did. We trace our family history and tape record and Video-tape our elders, so as to have memory of them.

Humans keep track of time. We use dates as markers for personal and public events that we recall. We remember not only the birthdays of families and friends, but also those of public figures who have died, like George Washington and Dr. Martin Luther King Jr. We observe Memorial Day to honor those who have died in the military and Independence Day to recall our birth as a nation. Animals don't celebrate such events. They don't keep records. History clearly shows humans to have a different way of knowing than sense, a mind which can remember and grasp the meaning of the past.

4. Humans are religious. They acknowledge the existence of a being higher than themselves. Humans devise rites of worship, compose prayers and hymns. Humans see themselves as responsible to a higher power and seek forgiveness from that power. In religion people find the answer to the question of their origin, their purpose in life, their final destiny. Religions express their beliefs in creeds and distinguish themselves from one another by these creeds. Humans recognize their helplessness before the forces of nature and the events of life, and look for help from an outside source in coping with their difficulties. Humans wear medals or charms, recite long prayers, and even fast, to seek such help. Animals have no religion, because they do not have intelligence capable of asking the questions about life's meaning as humans do. Nor do animals have the ability to create a belief system expressed in a creed, to organize rituals, to look for help beyond themselves.

5. Humans are professionals. We have the medical profession of doctors and nurses, and a host of specialists. We have the legal profession and the court system. We have teachers of elementary and high schools, of colleges and graduate schools; we have carpenters, plumbers, electricians, architects, we have social workers, firemen and policemen, elected legislators and executives. We have engineers and research scientists, artists and musicians. The list is endless. The root of this diversity is the ability of the human mind to grasp various aspects of reality, to see the

benefit of specialization, to recognize the different interests of humans, to grasp the necessity of standards for performance. The kind of specialization that humans do is of a far different character than the instinctive specialization of ants or bees in a colony. If humans had only their senses to guide them, they could never be doctors, lawyers, engineers or teachers. We do have a unique type of intelligence.

6. An additional indication of human intelligence is that humans create culture. A good deal of education is devoted to passing on the culture of a group, that cluster of beliefs, customs, and way of living specific to the group. Cultures have traditions, holidays and holydays, styles of eating and of clothing, etiquettes for regulating human interaction, entertainment events, such as sports, opera, drama, and musical concerts. Although the physical aspects of our being, and the physical world contribute significantly to culture, the meaning of culture comes from our minds. We use our bodies to shake hands, but the significance of shaking hands as a greeting is a product of intelligence. So, too, is the alternative form of greeting in many cultures, the bow. Clothes are made out of physical materials, but they are designed and produced by intelligence.

In sum, culture, like conscience, science, history, religion, and professionalism show that any theory of the human that limits the knowing ability of the human to what is sensed is seriously deficient, and that a moderate realist position recognizing the existence of a spiritual   power of knowing is not only viable, but necessary. Human intelligence is qualitatively different in kind than that of animals. It is unique.

FREEDOM

With regard to the essential trait of freedom, the moderate dualist position is called *voluntarism*, and supports the existence of free will. The materialist view on freedom, as we have seen, is *determinism*, and sees human actions as a product of a factor distinct from the will, whether biological, psychological or cultural in nature. We have already described the direct and indirect psychological argument for freedom and pointed out some of the flaws of the determinist position. Here we supplement our argument by considering three experiences of freedom: 1. the freedom of bodily control; 2. the freedom in speaking; and 3. the freedom to sacrifice for others. These three abilities point to an ability of self-determination not found in the animal kingdom.

1. With regard to bodily control, we can normally move arms and legs and fingers at will. More significantly, we can form a fist, or not, with our hand, leave it as it is normally, shape it to point out a direction to someone. We can walk or run or skip, and we can run or walk at varying speeds. We can put our body through exercises, standing erect, lying flat on our back, or sitting. We can throw a baseball or football, or shoot a basketball. We can dance: an Irish jig, a tango, the twist or the electric slide. We can become gymnasts and twirl our body on beams, or swing on poles. In all of these activities, we are directing our limbs to do something they do not instinctively do. Animals can be trained to do things like catch a Frisbee, or run in a race, but it is through application of physical rewards. No physical reward forces us to do push ups or run a marathon, or clap our hands in applause. We do these things freely, of our own volition, because we understand a purpose to those activities, a goal to be obtained by doing them.

2. The use of language also illustrates human freedom. Adult humans speak when they want to, whether at home, at work, or out in public. We also select what we will say, and how we will say it. If we are asking a favor from someone, we speak one way. If we are pointing out a fault, we express ourselves differently. We know how to praise others, ridicule them, or get them angry by our choice of words. We can give a friend or spouse "the silent treatment" and refuse to talk. We can bore others by talking constantly about ourselves, or we can get others to speak by asking them questions. We humans use words to entertain one another, to teach one another, to get information from one another—and we pick the words according to what it is we want to get or to know. Granted there are some close to compulsive talkers among us, but that fact does not change the fact that we do have the ability to control our speech. Animal communication is involuntary, arising from need instinctively, or sometimes through training.

3. Sacrifice is an act whereby we surrender something of our own to benefit another. A parent who takes an extra job to help pay for college tuition is making a sacrifice. A child who foregoes playing a favorite video game, and stays in to keep his sick brother or sister company is making a sacrifice. A fireman who runs into a burning building to save others is making a sacrifice, risking his life for others. Soldiers who stay at their posts and defend their country are making a sacrifice. People don't have to make sacrifices—parents can limit their children's choice of college to what they can afford; brothers and sisters can leave their siblings to watch television; firemen can be cautious and refuse to take a

chance; soldiers can desert their posts, or never sign up for the military in the first place. It is characteristic of humans to choose to give up something of their own to benefit others, and this is a behavior that humans esteem. Animals instinctively fight for their young, and pets have been known to respond to emergencies of their masters. But neither behavior is self-determined like the choice of one human to forego food so another may eat, or the rescue of a stranger from a fire by a fireman.

DUALITY

With regard to the composition of the human person, moderate dualists also stand on opposite sides from materialists. Moderate dualists see the human as a composite unity of a spiritual principle and a material principle, Materialists see the human as entirely a physical being, one whose entire behavior and life is the outcome of purely physical processes.

We have seen the evidence for a spiritual part of the human in looking at the intelligent activities of understanding, reasoning and self-consciousness, and the volitional activities of desiring what is non-material and the control of desire for a higher purpose. Our reflection on the activities of abstraction and language, games, art, technology and emotion has shown the close unity that exists between the mental and the physical.

Two additional human experiences can further support the moderate dualist position: 1. conscious non-verbal communication and 2.exercise.

1. Take the act of winking. When we are teasing a friend and saying something that we don't really mean, we indicate this to a bystander by a wink, a deliberate eye movement that the bystander understands to indicate that we are not speaking seriously. The desire to tease is accomplished by words, the desire to communicate that teasing is going on is communicated by a wink that clues bystanders to the teasing. The mental and the physical are at work in the non-verbal action of winking.

Also, when we wave at a person at a distance, salute, an officer, or signal someone to be silent by putting our hands to our lips, we are doing what is physical for a purpose that is non-physical, good neighborliness, or good manners. We are using both mind and body: mind, to apprehend the situation and to select the appropriate bodily gesture, and body, to carry out the action.

2. Exercise reveals our spiritual and physical nature. When I consciously do exercises to relieve back or neck stress, to flatten my abdo-

men, or to relax my eyes, I am moving my body in a way that will ac-
complish a purpose. Exercises are different from reflexes, because they
are purposeful, planned, executed freely. In addition, when I desire to
kick or throw a ball in a certain direction, much more than hand-eye coordination is required. I have to will the movement of my arms or leg,
have an idea of the direction I wish to throw or kick the ball, adapt the
effort of arm and leg so that the appropriate force, not one too great or
too little, is used. These activities are learned skills, as are winking and
shushing. They flow from intelligence, while they themselves involve
physical activity. Those actions are actions of a composite being with a
spiritual and a bodily component.

PERSON

When it comes to the human person, the moderate dualist holds to
the existence of a persistent self with spiritual powers of intellect and
will, abilities or powers of a spiritual soul. Contemporary materialists
seem to be as puzzled as Hume about the existence of a self, and look for
physiological or social origins to explain the self.[4] Three features of human life and experience argue for a persistent individual self: 1. practice;
2. pretense; and 3. courts.

1. From our youth, we learn that "practice makes perfect." We repeat hitting or throwing a ball, reciting a poem, jumping over a rope, or
whatever. We have rehearsals for plays and speeches, parades and formal
ceremonies like weddings and graduations. The persistent self must be
the one learning the skill practiced or rehearsed. Furthermore, sometimes
we impose these rehearsals and practices on ourselves—say our lines
over and over in front of a mirror, take extra batting practice, or keep
juggling the cards till we master the trick. We are conscious of ourselves
when we rehearse, and we rehearse and practice because we want to perform well, to please not only others, but ourselves.

2. "Let's Pretend" was a radio show of the Fifties. Pretending is a
special human trait. Animals can play dead and hide for protection, but
only humans pretend to be lost and play hide and seek. Humans create
plays in which people pretend to be mad, glad, or sad. People pretend to
be angry to impress or convince others. People pretend to be drunk in
order to amuse others. People wear costumes and pretend they are a soldier, or a princess. People pretend not to be interested in someone they

are attracted to. In order to pretend to be other than you are, you must have an awareness of who you are.

3. The legal systems of nations are predicated on the continuity of personal identity. It must be the same perpetrator that comes to trial six months or a year later, who was first charged. Outside the legal system, we have the "court of public opinion," which again presupposes the identity of the doer of deeds one has witnessed or heard about. And there is the "court" of one's own conscience, condemning or approving of what the self has done. An argument from the first two "courts" easily fits into a common consent argument:

The human race cannot be wrong about a universally held, important belief.

Humans universally believe in personal identity and that concept is important.

Therefore, the human race cannot be wrong about the belief in personal identity.

All these considerations suggest that personal identity as a persistent self is so evident it belongs among the presuppositions of Philosophy, not as an item to be discussed. How could anyone dialogue or have meaningful dialogue with a self that was just a group of impressions?

IMMORTALITY

When it comes to the topic of immortality, the gap between moderate dualists and materialists is as wide as it could be. The latter, seeing nothing non-physical in humans, view death as the end of everything. The former, convinced of the spiritual component in humans, argue for personal immortality. The difficulty of arriving at a definitive proof of the issue was acknowledged long ago by Plato, who, nevertheless, stated that it was too important an issue not to take a stand on.[5] Scotus, in the thirteenth century, held that immortality could not be demonstrated philosophically, but that persuasive reasons for it could be given.[6] In the eighteenth century, Kant argued that immortality, like the existence of God and freedom, could not be proved—or disproved.[7] Evaluating these different opinions would carry us into a discussion of standards of proof, epistemological and metaphysical assumptions, and also involve taking a large dose of the history of philosophy. The reader will have to make up his or her own mind, perhaps with help from outside the realm of philosophy.

SIDE TAKEN

From the foregoing exposition, it emerges that moderate dualism is proposed as the most coherent Philosophy of the Human Being. This position seems closest to human experience, human tradition, and human hopes. The free, social and intelligent, dual, and individual nature of the human being is close to intuitive knowledge. In a real sense we have discussed in this course "what everybody knows." Consideration of opposing views serves to confirm this intuition, at least from this author's point of view. A by-product of our reflections, we hope, is an understanding of what philosophy is, how philosophers go about their work, and a facility for thinking things through.

NOTES

1. Desmond Morris, *The Naked Ape. A Zoologist's Study of the Human Animal* (New York: McGraw-Hill, 1967).
2. See Azar, op. *cit.*, chapter 13.
3. See Gonsalves, *op. cit.*, c. 4, 48-64.
4. See for example, Thomas Nagel "Brain Bisection and the Unity of Consciousness," and Kenneth J. Gergen, "The Social Construction of Self-Consciousness," in Daniel Kolak and Raymond Martin. *Self and Identity: Contemporary Philosophical Issues* (New York: Macmillan, 1991).
5. Plato, *Phaedo,* 85.
6. Scotus, *op. cit.*, 156-58. See note 9 Chapter 7.
7. Immanuel Kant, *Critique of Practical Reason* II, 142-149.

Appendix

DEFINITION AND RULES OF DEFINITION[1]

DEFINITION

Definition: the explanation of the meaning of a term.

Nominal definition: the explanation of the meaning of a term by giving its literal or etymological or root meaning. Example: An astronaut is a star sailor.

Real Definition: the explanation of the actual or factual meaning of the term. Example: An astronaut is a human who travels in a space capsule outside the atmosphere of the earth.

Stipulative definition: any chosen or selected meaning. Example: By the word "argument" in philosophy, we mean a logical proof of something based on compelling reasons.

Essential definition: an explanation of the very nature or being of something, through genus (a wider class) and difference (a feature that makes a kind of thing distinct from other types of thing in that class). Example: Humans are rational (difference) animals (genus).

RULES OF DEFINITION

1. *Definition should be coextensive with what is being defined, not too wide or too narrow.*

Violation: Philosophy of the human person is the study of men and women. This definition is clearly too wide, since other branches of

---

1. See Patrick J. Hurley. *A Concise Introduction to Logic.* Eighth Edition. (Belmont, CA: Wadsworth Publishing Co., 2003), 104-107.

knowledge study men and women, anthropology, psychology, sociology, biology.

Violation: Philosophy of the human person is the study of human freedom and intelligence. This definition is too narrow, since philosophy of the human person also studies human sociability, duality, individuality, and immortality.

2. *Definition should not be circular:* It should go beyond the literal meaning of the term, and should not use a word just like it.

Violation: Philosophy is the love of wisdom.

Violation: Materialism is the view that everything is material.

3. *Definition should be positive, when possible.*

Violation: Philosophy is a branch of knowledge which is not science. (Also too broad, since religion is also a branch of knowledge which is not science.)

Not a violation: Involuntary means not willingly.

4. *Definition should not be expressed in vague, obscure or figurative language.*

Violation: Philosophy is the study of things hard to define.

Violation: Philosophy is the transcendent study of transcendence.

5. *Definition should give the essential meaning of what is defined.*

Violation: Language is a trait that distinguishes humans from animals.

Violation: Intelligence is the ability to ask questions.

6. *Definition should be expressed in proper grammatical form.*

Violation: Materialism is when we say the human is made of only physical parts.

7. *Definition should indicate its context.*

Violation: Term means a word with meaning. It should read: "a term, in philosophy, means a word with meaning."

Note: TRUE STATEMENTS ABOUT THINGS ARE NOT THEREBY DEFINITIONS.

BIBLIOGRAPHY

Adler, Mortimer. *Ten Philosophical Mistakes*. (New York: Macmillan, 1985).

―――. *The Difference in Man and the Difference It Makes*. (New York: Holt, Rinehart and Winston, 1967).

A.J. Ayer and Raymond Winch, Edd. *British Empirical Philosophers*. (New York: Simon and Schuster, 1968).

Aquinas, Thomas. *The Soul; A Translation of St. Thomas Aquinas' De anima*. John P. Rowan. (St. Louis: B. Herder Co., 1949).

―――. *Summa Theologica*. Trans. Dominican Fathers. 3 Vol. (New York: Benziger Brs., 1947).

Aristotle. *The Collected Works of Aristotle*. The Revised Oxford Translation. Ed. Jonathan Barnes. 2 Vol. (Princeton, NJ: Princeton University Press, 1984).

Azar, Larry. *Man: Computer, Ape or Angel?* (Hanover, MA: Christopher Publishing Co., 1989).

Berkeley, George. *On the Principles of Human Knowledge*. Philosophical Writings. (New York: Greenwood Press, 1969).

Donceel, Joseph, S.J. *Philosophical Anthropology*. (New York: Sheed and Ward, 1969).

Flew, Antony. Ed. *Body, Mind and Death*. (New York: Macmillan, 1964).

Harvey, Rudolf. *It Stands to Reason*. (New York: Joseph F. Wagner, Inc., 1960).

Hobbes, Thomas. *Leviathan*. (London: Dent, 1973).

Hume, David. *A Treatise of Human Nature*. (Oxford: Clarendon Press, 1888).

―――. *An Enquiry Concerning Human Understanding*. (Chicago: Regnery, 1965).

Hurley, Patrick J. *A Concise Introduction to Logic*. Eighth Edition: (Belmont, CA: Wadsworth Publishing Co.), 2003.

Koren, Henry. *An Introduction to the Philosophy of Animate Nature*. (St. Louis: B. Herder, 1955).

Kreeft, Peter. *The Best Things in Life*. (Downers Grove, IL: Intervarsity Press, 1984).

Kreyche, G. and Mann, J. Edd. *Perspectives on Reality*. (New York: Harcourt, Brace and World, 1966).

Lewis, C.S. *The Problem of Pain*. (New York: Macmillan, 1948).

————. *The Pilgrim's Regress*. (London: Geoffrey Bles, 1935).

Lucretius, *Of the Nature of Things*. Trans. W.E. Leonard. (New York: Dutton, 1957).

Marcel, Gabriel. *Homo Viator: An Introduction to the Metaphysics of Hope*. Trans. Francis Cornford. (Chicago: Regnery, 1957).

Peters, John. *Metaphysics: A Systematic Study*. (Pittsburgh: Duquesne University Press, 1963).

Plato. *The Collected Dialogues of Plato*. Edd. Hamilton and Cairns, (New York: Bollingen Foundation, 1961).

Reichmann, James, S.J. *The Philosophy of the Human Person*. (Chicago: Loyola University Press, 1985).

Rice, Charles. *Fifty Questions on Natural Law*. (San Francisco: Ignatius Press, 1993).

Sartre, John Paul. *Being and Nothingness*. Trans. Hazel Barnes. (New York: Philosophical Library, 1965).

Skinner, B.F. *Beyond Freedom and Dignity*, (New York: Knopf, 1971).

Suzuki, David and Knudson, Peter. *Genethics*. (Cambridge, MA: Harvard University Press, 1960).

Wilson, E.O. *On Human Nature*. (Cambridge, MA: Harvard University Press, 1978).

INDEX

ABOUT THE AUTHOR

REV. JULIAN A. DAVIES, O.F.M. is a native of Utica, New York. He was ordained to the priesthood in 1960 and received his Ph.D. in Philosophy from Fordham University in 1970. He has taught at Siena College, Loudonville, New York since that time and has been Professor of Philosophy since 1984.

CPSIA information can be obtained
at www.ICGtesting.com
Printed in the USA
BVHW030846260820
587340BV00001B/81

9 780761 845164